Kenneth E. Eble 1923–1988

NEW DIRECTIONS FOR TEACHING AND LEARNING

Robert E. Young, *University of Wisconsin*
EDITOR-IN-CHIEF

Excellent Teaching in a Changing Academy: Essays in Honor of Kenneth Eble

Feroza Jussawalla
University of Texas, El Paso

EDITOR

Number 44, Winter 1990

JOSSEY-BASS INC., PUBLISHERS
San Francisco

EXCELLENT TEACHING IN A CHANGING ACADEMY: ESSAYS IN HONOR OF
KENNETH EBLE
Feroza Jussawalla (ed.)
New Directions for Teaching and Learning, no. 44
Robert E. Young, Editor-in-Chief

© 1990 by Jossey-Bass Inc., Publishers. All rights reserved.

No part of this issue may be reproduced in any form—except for a brief quotation (not to exceed 500 words) in a review or professional work—without permission in writing from the publishers.

Microfilm copies of issues and articles are available in 16mm and 35mm, as well as microfiche in 105mm, through University Microfilms Inc., 300 North Zeeb Road, Ann Arbor, Michigan 48106.

LC 85-644763   ISSN 0271-0633   ISBN 1-55542-818-5

NEW DIRECTIONS FOR TEACHING AND LEARNING is part of The Jossey-Bass Higher and Adult Education Series and is published quarterly by Jossey-Bass Inc., Publishers. Second-class postage paid at San Francisco, California, and at additional mailing offices. Postmaster: Send address changes to Jossey-Bass Inc., Publishers, 350 Sansome Street, San Francisco, California 94104.

EDITORIAL CORRESPONDENCE should be sent to Jossey-Bass Inc., Publishers, 350 Sansome Street, San Francisco, California 94104.

Cover photograph by Richard Blair/Color & Light © 1990.

Printed on acid-free paper in the United States of America.

Contents

PREFACE 1
David Pierpont Gardner

ABOUT KENNETH EBLE 3

EDITOR'S NOTES 5
Feroza Jussawalla

1. The Degradation of Undergraduate Education 11
Kenneth Eble
In creating a research university rated in terms of "star faculty" and research output, teaching is ignored.

2. The Art of Deliberalizing: A Handbook for the True Professional 21
Wayne C. Booth
"Yoomwreck," a hypothetical institution, tries to soar in the universities' ratings game.

3. The Transforming of the American Mind 33
Henry Louis Gates, Jr.
Incorporating minority studies and culturally diverse points of view is imperative for higher education.

4. Miss Grimp Revisited: Reconfiguring Composition, Literature, and Cultural Literacy 45
Feroza Jussawalla
Teaching cultural diversity need not be political and can lead to an increased awareness of Western cultural heritage.

5. A Coaching Model for the Teaching of Writing 53
Anthony J. Walsh
The coaching model offers valuable insight into how such skills as writing are learned, polished, and finally applied under pressure.

6. The Politics of the Classroom: Toward an Oppositional Pedagogy 61
Minette Marcroft
In the current conservative climate of higher education, questioning students' political beliefs is imperative for a real democratization of knowledge.

7. The Lower End of Higher Education: Freshmen, Sophomores, 73
the Research University, and the Community College
Timothy R. Bywater
Universities often fall short in dealing with freshmen and sophomores; community colleges offer great potential for teaching these students.

8. What Good Are Computers in the Writing Classroom? 83
Michael Dobberstein
The use of computers alone cannot perceptibly improve student writing.

9. Encouraging and Evaluating Scholarship for the College Teacher 91
Paul A. Lacey
While publishing has until now been the sole form of scholarship rewarded, alternative forms should be encouraged and used in evaluating faculty.

10. Kenneth Eble on Writing in College: Ahead of His Time 101
William J. McCleary
Eble's positions on the term paper, writing across the curriculum, and learning through writing are discussed.

11. The Bush Foundation's Faculty Development Projects 107
Humphrey Doermann
Faculty development grants that encourage teamwork are more productive than isolated grants for scholarship.

INDEX 115

Preface

"I have spent my life quarreling with my profession," Kenneth Eble (1976) once wrote, "an impossible way to live, I think, except that I have won some and lost some and moved the immovable even as I am dismayed at how little that movement was" (p. 166). As teacher, scholar, administrator, and author—to name the principal outlets for Eble's abundant energies—he actually quarreled with several professions and brought to every argument passion, dedication, clear thinking, and broad imagination. Yet it was for the craft of teaching that he reserved his most creative thinking and his deepest commitment.

I became acquainted with Ken Eble during my ten years as president of the University of Utah. I came to admire and respect not only his many-faceted scholarship and his professional skills but especially his dedication to the improvement of undergraduate education. Thanks to his writings, his lectures, and his willingness to share his stock of teaching experience, his influence spread in ever-widening circles throughout the nation and beyond, transcending his field of American literature and even the humanities to shape the practice of teaching in many disciplines and in primary and secondary schools as well as in colleges and universities. His efforts were always on behalf of innovation, on ways to make learning come dramatically alive, and countless teachers—novice and seasoned alike—have benefited from his wise and practical advice about what he called "the particulars of teaching."

The philosophy of teaching he both embraced and lived is of profound significance today. Some years ago I chaired the National Commission on Excellence in Education, whose 1983 report, *A Nation at Risk*, helped launch a national movement to reform our schools. Everything we learned during the course of our work underscored the fundamental importance—indeed, the urgency—of inspired teaching not just in the nation's high schools but at all levels of education.

In recent years a number of national reports (Boyer, 1988; Study Group . . . , 1984) have raised serious questions about the quality of undergraduate education and especially the quality of undergraduate teaching. My own view is not that we are doing such a bad job overall but that we could be doing so much better; the national interest generated by these reports raises the welcome prospect of a renewed concern about and attention to enhancing the educational experience of undergraduates at our colleges and universities. Improvement of the kind we need will require many kinds of support: financial, administrative, and moral. Above all, it will require the kind of intense dedication and personal involvement in the daily realities of teaching that characterized Eble and his work over many years.

This book in his honor pays him the compliment of continuing the journey along paths he first explored. In the words of his beloved Thoreau ([1854] 1973), "if one advances confidently in the direction of his dreams, and endeavors to live the life which he has imagined, he will meet with a success unexpected in common hours" (p. 323).

Ken Eble was an individual whose talent and imagination touched many lives and opened to them vistas that might otherwise have remained closed. This volume celebrates a remarkably creative and successful life, one dedicated to the proposition that what goes on in the classroom is of deep and lasting significance not just for the individuals involved but for our society. I am pleased to commend it to the reader.

David Pierpont Gardner

References

Boyer, E. *College: The Undergraduate Experience in America.* New York: Harper & Row, 1988.

Eble, K. E. *The Craft of Teaching: A Guide to Mastering the Professor's Art.* San Francisco: Jossey-Bass, 1976.

National Commission on Excellence in Education. "A Nation at Risk: The Imperative for Educational Reform." *Chronicle of Higher Education,* May 4, 1983, pp. 11–14.

Study Group on the Condition of Excellence in Higher Education. *Involvement in Learning: Realizing the Potential of American Higher Education.* Final Report. Washington, D.C.: U.S. Department of Education, 1984.

Thoreau, H. D. *Walden.* Princeton, N.J.: Princeton University Press, 1973. (Originally published 1854.)

David Pierpont Gardner is president of the University of California.

About Kenneth Eble

Kenneth E. Eble was professor of English and University Professor at the University of Utah, Salt Lake City. He received his bachelor's and master's degrees from the University of Iowa (1948, 1949) and his doctorate in English from Columbia University (1956).

Eble began teaching at Upper Iowa University in 1949, and he taught at the Columbia School of General Studies (1951-54) and Drake University (1954-55) before joining the faculty at the University of Utah in 1955. He served as visiting professor in American studies at Carleton College (1967), directed seminars in college teaching for the Colombian Ministry of Education (1975) and the Kansas City Regional Council for Higher Education (1976), and was Visiting Robinson Professor at George Mason University (1986).

From 1964 to 1969, he was chair of the English department at the University of Utah, taking leave from 1969 to 1971 to direct the Project to Improve College Teaching, cosponsored by the American Association of University Professors (AAUP) and the Association of American Colleges and funded by the Carnegie Corporation. In 1973, he was awarded an honorary Doctor of Humane Letters from Saint Francis College (Biddeford, Maine) and was Distinguished Visiting Scholar for the Educational Testing Service in 1973-74.

For more than twenty years, Eble was a guest speaker and consultant on teaching and faculty development at more than 200 colleges and universities in the United States and Canada. He served in many official positions within the AAUP, the Modern Language Association, the National Council of Teachers of English, and Phi Beta Kappa. He served on the board of directors of the American Association for Higher Education from 1983 to 1986 and was named to the advisory board of the National Center for Research to Improve Postsecondary Teaching and Learning in 1986. He was one of ten finalists for the Council for Advancement and Support of Education's Professor of the Year in 1985.

Eble's writing has embraced not only education but American literature, the humanities, the history of ideas, and popular culture as well. In addition to *Professors as Teachers* (Jossey-Bass, 1972), *The Aims of College Teaching* (Jossey-Bass, 1983), *The Art of Administration* (Jossey-Bass, 1978), and *Improving Undergraduate Education Through Faculty Development* (with Wilbert McKeachie, Jossey-Bass, 1985), Eble's books include *William Dean*

This is adapted from "The Author" in K. E. Eble, *The Craft of Teaching: A Guide to Mastering the Professor's Art* (2nd ed.), San Francisco: Jossey-Bass, 1988.

Howells (Twayne, 1982), *F. Scott Fitzgerald* (revised edition, Twayne, 1976), and *Old Clemens and W.D.H.* (Louisiana State University, 1985). He edited *Howells: A Century of Criticism* (Southern Methodist University, 1962), *The Intellectual Tradition of the West* (Scott, Foresman, 1967), and *F. Scott Fitzgerald: A Collection* (McGraw-Hill, 1973). He was a field editor for the Twayne United States Author Series and edited *New Directions for Teaching and Learning* for Jossey-Bass from 1980 to 1988.

Editor's Notes

Today's institutions compete in the ratings game by buying so-called star faculty; by rewarding only research, publications, and grant writing; and by hiring token minority candidates to present a veneer of cultural diversity. Often, in this changed atmosphere, teaching is acknowledged only through computerized student questionnaires by means of which professors are made to compete in a popularity game, much as television game-show hosts must compete in the Nielsen ratings.

When an "upwardly mobile" state university's English department chair wrote to the *Chronicle of Higher Education* about his ambition to make his department as prestigious as that of the University of Virginia, Kenneth Eble, always quick to respond to what he thought were superfluities in academia, replied with a letter that pointed out the foolishness of such a goal. This is just one example of how, as the academy changed, Eble poked fun at its pretensions. As a true sixties radical, he had been part of the movement that fostered academic change, a movement that pushed for more relaxed teaching styles, for more student feedback in the curriculum, for innovations in the way teaching was evaluated, and above all for the maintenance of an ethical stance in the classroom. During the eighties, as an increased conservatism overtook an academy more and more oriented toward research, Eble's activism took the form of deploring such developments as the dictatorial pronouncements on curricula and on the general nature of the academy that were being made by both right- and left-wing politicians and university administrators. Because of his own liberal views, he objected to the conservative curricula proposed by those on the right, but he also disagreed with the new postmodern left, identifying it with a form of elitism that ignores undergraduate education.

One of my own experiences with Eble illustrates his antielitist sentiments. In the spring of 1988, I had just returned home from an interview at a small liberal arts college in Texas. Since Eble had been the second reader for my dissertation on a topic that had by 1988 become fashionable—third world literature (although it was not so fashionable when I wrote my dissertation)—I called him up to lament the fact that he had not made me use the vocabulary of a more theoretical literary criticism. The people on the interviewing committee, though interested in my work, had wanted it expressed in the academically fashionable language of postmodern theory. In addition, the interviewers had been disappointed that I was not suitably exotic enough. "If you're really a minority, why is your skin so white?" I had been asked. They were searching for a visible minority to hire so that they could get matching funds from their administration. Finally, the committee had complained about the tenured assistant professors who did not publish and who supposedly concentrated only on teaching. The road to tenure, the committee members warned, was paved with publications. Those who did not publish, especially with the new fashionable presses and in the new theoretical journals, were labeled the "petrified forest."

This experience, I felt, encapsulated the changes that had overtaken the academy by 1988, and these changes were what I bemoaned to Eble. In response to my phone call, Eble prepared the following letter:

> Association for the Sane Study of Literature
>
> Dear Colleague:
>
> The time has come, the walrus said, to form an Association for the Sane Study of Literature. It will cost you $1 and a twenty-five-cent stamp to mail a letter expressing your interest. This is a test mailing. If there is a wave of support, your dollar will do something to make the wave visible. If there is no wave, then your dollar has gone to hell for sure and probably literature with it. The dollar isn't important anyhow. What is is a willingness to support some simple, sane beliefs about the study of literature.
>
> If you believe that literature is a source of great pleasure and that enchancing that pleasure for students is a primary purpose of literary study, then this organization should appeal to you.
>
> If you believe that poetry and fiction and drama are primary and that criticism by any name is secondary, then join up.
>
> If you wince at words like "privileging," "problematize," "reify," "bracketing," "signifying," "intertextuality," and find a phrase like "to foreground the problematics of the discipline" both pompous and ugly, put up your dollar.
>
> If you've always thought that literature should have social contexts but get a bit irritated at the notion that it can only be approached through theories of race, class, and gender, then it may be worth your time to reply.
>
> If, for that matter, you think literary theories are less interesting and valuable than poems, plays, and stories, respond. . . .
>
> This association has no charter or officers or stationery or even headquarters. If you want to be an officer, send $2 and state your preference of office. If you want to hold a convention, name the time and place. If you want to set out your views in readable prose, do it, and at least one person will read it.
>
> Can you get more than this for a dollar? There is no establishment, group, interpretive community, shadowy figure, right- or left-wing coterie behind this—just me and the English teacher friend who urged me to do it.

Although Eble's satire here was aimed at English departments in particular, he was equally critical of the elitism that is beginning to permeate all of higher education.

Much attention has been focused on Lynne Cheney's (1989) and

Allan Bloom's (1987) call to "deliberalize" the academy à la Hirsch (1987) and Bennett (1984). But the battle lines do not simply divide those who are liberal from those who are not, as Eble's views illustrate. One of Eble's students, Fred Moramarco (1988), noted in his memorial essay that Eble "agreed with F. Scott Fitzgerald, an author he wrote about with grace and insight, that the test of a first-rate intellect is the ability to hold two opposed ideas in the mind at the same time and still retain the ability to function."

In this spirit, then, this volume seeks not to resolve the issues surrounding academia today but rather to mark the contested points in the debates on whether to incorporate cultural diversity in the curriculum, whether to compete for the research dollar, and how to evaluate faculty humanely in a changing atmosphere. It is imperative that we find ways to foster good teaching and learning in an academy that must change to meet the needs of students from different demographic backgrounds and with different levels of preparedness, an academy that is facing continuing political and budgetary pressures. This is what Eble urged; as Moramarco explained:

> Instead of blaming the troubles of universities on students and the relativistic curriculum as Bloom does, Ken stressed the way teaching has been devalued over the years as universities compete for the big dollars and big prestige which everyone knows is in research. This is the point Ken made in different forms over the past two decades, and though its truth is patently obvious, the university community in this country continues to deny it, looking, like an alcoholic family, elsewhere for its woes.

The chapters in this volume have been chosen to honor Eble's insight. In Chapter One (which was prepared as a talk and is published here for the first time), Eble spells out the changes he saw occurring in the academy. In Chapter Two, Wayne C. Booth captures the spirit of the Eble-like response to these changes that many faculty are beginning to have. His chapter also embodies the light-hearted tone in which Eble usually conveyed his positions, and for this reason, I asked Booth if I could reproduce the chapter here. Similarly, I asked Henry Louis Gates, Jr., for Chapter Three, which was presented as a talk at the University of Texas at El Paso (UTEP) on March 8, 1990, because I felt it spoke eloquently to the concerns Eble had about the Bloomian conservatism overtaking the academy. Gates argues that cultural diversity must be included, not superficially, but in every aspect of the academic curriculum.

A number of chapters in this volume are written by Eble's former students. These chapters reflect the ways in which the writers have expanded on Eble's teaching in their own work. For example, in Chapter Four, I describe how something as unorthodox as incorporating third world literature in the composition classroom can be helpful to students. My experience reveals how teaching can be enhanced by overcoming political confrontations within departments.

Chapter Five is by a reader of Eble's work, Anthony J. Walsh. He describes how Eble's loving, nurturing approach can be implemented in the classroom.

The next three chapters are written by students of Kenneth Eble like myself. In Chapter Six, Minette Marcroft urges engagement in political confrontations as the only way to maintain a truly democratic classroom. This chapter is essentially the antithesis of the preceding one and shows how Marcroft's work, though it has grown away from Eble's teaching techniques, still retains a concern for education as an equalizing force. In Chapter Seven, Timothy R. Bywater shows how the community college fosters learning despite Bloomian elitism. In Chapter Eight, Michael Dobberstein writes the perfect complement to Eble's (1986) "Word Processors: Zucchini in the Academic Garden." The chapter surveys studies on whether computers can help students learn how to write.

Chapters Nine, Ten, and Eleven are retrospective chapters written by Eble's colleagues. In Chapter Nine, Paul A. Lacey addresses Eble's work on faculty evaluation and points to humane ways of evaluating faculty. In Chapter Ten, William J. McCleary outlines Eble's work in teaching composition, and in Chapter Eleven, Humphrey Doermann describes Eble's participation in the Bush Foundation's faculty development projects. All eleven chapters provide new directions for excellent teaching in a changing academy.

Acknowledgments

I am grateful to Mrs. Peggy Eble for her support from my first suggestion of this project. She has been of invaluable assistance in contacting people associated with Ken and in searching for materials important in preparing this manuscript. Thanks are also due to Melissa Eble-Tuller for her help, to David Hackett of the UTEP History department for help in converting various software packages, and to the computer center's staff for their help with the optical scanner. As always, my husband Reed Dasenbrock waited patiently and helped with the details of editing and formatting.

This book is dedicated to the excellent teachers I have known: Kenneth Eble, William Mulder, Reed, and my mother, a university professor and administrator. As Eble (1988) wrote, "The scholar-teacher who combines both types is a recognizable figure as well as an anomalous one" (p. 19). Wayne Booth and Henry Louis Gates, along with the other contributors to this volume, also fit this model, and I am grateful to them for the inclusion of their chapters here.

Feroza Jussawalla
Editor

References

Bennett, W. J. " 'To Reclaim a Legacy': Text of Report on Humanities in Education." *Chronicle of Higher Education,* November 28, 1984, pp. 16-22.

Bloom, A. *The Closing of the American Mind.* New York: Simon & Schuster, 1987.

Cheney, L. V. *Fifty Hours: A Core Curriculum for College Students.* Washington, D.C.: National Endowment for the Humanities, 1989.

Eble, K. E. "Word Processors: Zucchini in the Academic Garden." *Chronicle of Higher Education,* July 16, 1986, p. A16.

Eble, K. E. *The Craft of Teaching: A Guide to Mastering the Professor's Art.* (2nd ed.) San Francisco: Jossey-Bass, 1988.

Hirsch, E. D., Jr. *Cultural Literacy: What Every American Needs to Know.* Boston: Houghton Mifflin, 1987.

Moramarco, F. "In Memoriam." Essay written to be read at Kenneth Eble's memorial service, Salt Lake City, Utah, October 1988.

Feroza Jussawalla is associate professor of English and director of the honors program at the University of Texas at El Paso.

The increased emphasis on research and grantsmanship leaves professors with little time or inclination for undergraduate teaching.

The Degradation of Undergraduate Education

Kenneth Eble

> For the teachers and scholars I prize, there will always be conflicting demands. Early in our careers, I think, we do some things—formal scholarship, for example—so that we might gain the freedom and respectability to do others—raise our voices about teaching, for example.
> —Eble, 1988.

By this time, I think enough has been said about Allan Bloom's (1987) book. It is a tract for its time, the academic equivalent of TV evangelism, and matches the sanctimony, certitude, and straining for effect of this genre. The reasons for the book getting so much attention have also been worked over thoroughly. Already it is experiencing the diminished celebrity of Robert Bork, both prime examples of the right wing's need to claim an intellectual or two, though one might think that William Buckley constitutes superfluity in himself.

It is an oddity of my own experiencing of momentary fame that I have a group picture taken in November 1965 of participants in a public affairs conference at the University of Chicago. There I am between Charles Percy, U.S. Senator from Illinois, and Ed Magnusson, then education editor of *Time*, next to him Allan Bloom, then assistant professor at Chicago, next to him James Bryant Conant, president of Harvard, and so on.

This chapter was prepared as a talk and delivered in a symposium on Allan Bloom's *The Closing of the American Mind*, July 27, 1988, at San Diego State University.

In reflecting on that occasion, on Bloom's present book, and on my twenty-five years as an academic in between, I think we have arrived at a place where a concern for education has pretty much given way to a concern for power.

Taking a longer view, I would say that such a direction was perceived by Henry Adams ([1918] 1974) and made visible in his time by the patterning of American higher education after the German university. Closer to the present, I date this development from the expansion of higher education after World War II and its linkage with the military-industrial complex. American expansion has always been linked with power, and the sixties were a great period for academic hustling—buildings going up, faculties being created, legislators wooed, donors enshrined, grants pursued. Had it not been for the temporary displacements of civil rights and feminism, the Vietnam War and student unrest, we would probably have gotten to where we are now somewhat sooner.

And where are we now? We are at a place where higher education is but distantly connected with shaping a citizenry, where a general upward mobility is replaced by a narrower grasping for status and wealth, and where undergraduate education has become largely irrelevant because, in itself, it gives little promise of either.

The Flight from Teaching

Since I know most about faculty and the institutions in which they operate, I will begin there, with some concrete particulars about the faculty relationship to undergraduate education. In 1964, the Carnegie Foundation issued a report describing what it called "the flight from teaching." The report expressed concern about the ability of graduate schools to produce enough college teachers, but it also cited other factors that "diminish the use we are getting of those who are now in the ranks of teachers." Foremost among these factors was the presence and attraction of funded research, which had grown from $74 million in 1940 to almost $15 billion in 1964. (In 1985, $34 million went to thirty universities for "Star Wars" research alone. The total for Department of Defense research in 1987 was $1.463 billion.) Faculty were also being drawn off by a corresponding rise in consulting opportunities with government and industry. Teaching hours were undergoing a general reduction despite the increasing numbers of students. In "eminent" universities, average teaching loads were estimated at six hours for teachers in the sciences and 8.3 for those in the humanities.

What was observed as a flight then, chiefly affecting the rarer academic birds, has now become a mass migration. No one wants to teach freshmen, a few will condescend to take on sophomores if they happen to be promising majors, but most will seek out graduate courses or will shape undergraduate courses to their own graduate school preoccupations. The flight, I should add, extends beyond higher education. Teaching has rarely had a compelling hold on many of its practitioners. In the public schools for most of this century, women were the ones who took on this responsibility. For men, the route of flight from teaching took them into school administration. With the growth of colleges and universities after World War II, increasing numbers of men (and more women, although still fewer than men) opted for college and university teaching. The expanding community college system became a way up for both men and women who felt themselves overworked, underpaid, and little respected as public school teachers. What the Carnegie Foundation was describing was simply an internal flight within an expanding system of higher education: away from lower-division classes, away from general education, away from teaching at all if it could be avoided by seizing research and other opportunities. The long and short of the matter is that American society has never supported well the large numbers of teachers needed to teach many basic subjects to even larger numbers of students. Undergraduate education is experiencing what the public schools experienced long ago: a steady decline in the status of, compensation for, and commitment to teaching. In those areas where there is still a market for professors—science, technology, and business, for instance—the talented and ambitious set their sights on university careers in which teaching will be subordinated to their rise as disciplinary scholars. In those areas in which there is lesser demand—the humanities and social sciences—increasing numbers of the most able choose to pursue advanced studies that lead to careers of a more lucrative kind: law, medicine, and business administration.

While there are fluctuations over time in choice of careers, the trend seems clear: away from teaching itself, whether in lower or upper schools, as witnessed by the coming faculty shortages. Perhaps the trend is inevitable: Both Henry Adams and William James found teaching a heavy burden (though James and Adams are hardly to be compared with present-day college faculty), and as college professing expanded beyond the role of teaching, so did some aspects of its attractiveness. Colleges and universities are still places of privilege, and a substantial work force can enjoy a nine-month occupation with a great deal of individual autonomy. If physical facilities have not quite kept up with corporate headquarters, they are at least on a par with most shopping malls. And while salaries are a source of chronic complaint, the lazy can still earn more than they are probably worth and the talented and ambitious profit under highly competitive conditions.

Reasons Teachers Fly

The May–June 1988 issue of *Academe* devoted its contents to "Whatever Happened to 'The Faculty?'" To keep my own analysis within bounds, I'll draw on those contents. The main articles point to rising salary differences within the university, to the growth of the "superstar" system, to the increasing employment and exploitation of part-time faculty, and to the conflicts between specialized disciplinary interests and those of higher education. All of these have adverse effects on faculty responsible for undergraduate education. Salary differences favor those teaching graduate courses in institutions with strong graduate programs, just as they disfavor those teaching in the lower division and outside disciplines. Superstars invariably are identified by their achievements as researchers or practitioners rather than as teachers, and few give any substantial portion of their time to undergraduate teaching. As to part-time faculty, the writers (members of the staff of the Modern Language Association) warn, "an increasingly large, haphazardly gathered faculty is on the point of becoming a permanent part of the instructional staff for a substantial proportion of the undergraduate students our departments are responsible for teaching" (Franklin, Laurence, and Denham, 1988, p. 18). Finally, the concern over the dominance of specialized disciplinary interests is an acknowledgment of how extensively and tightly the "Ph.D. octopus" described by William James in 1907 has spread and wound its tentacles.

I have written about most of these matters for almost three decades now, and I will be brief in adding something to them. Clearly, the changing nature of the faculty has diminished the commitment to undergraduate teaching. More faculty in more institutions have pulled away from lower-division work. More teaching assistants and part-time instructors carry the bulk of teaching in basic courses, particularly in mathematics and composition. More of the content and preoccupations of graduate study have been brought down into what actual teaching faculty members are obliged to do. Far more concern and commitment are given to department majors and graduate students than to any student's overall undergraduate education.

Full-time professors have made an increasingly smaller commitment to undergraduate teaching for at least three decades. This is not merely a matter of reducing teaching loads and avoiding lower levels of teaching but constitutes a withdrawal from concerns with or commitments to undergraduate education. Outside pressures (the numerous reports critical of undergraduate education) and perhaps tradition ("the college experience" still has a favorable ring useful to attracting donors) probably account for what survives as liberal or general education. But the debates on that subject have pretty much degenerated into the claim that what is good for a department major is good for the university. It took a flood of foreign cars to dispel the similar notion that what was good for General Motors was good for the country. The college curriculum will continue to be, at best, the result of compromises reached among departments contending that a certain number of their specialized courses are vital for a student's undergraduate education.

Research Versus Teaching

The faculty's flight from teaching is in part an adaptive survival mechanism likely to arise among any endangered species. The research universities occupy the top of the higher education hierarchy and thereby shape all behavior in the four-year institutions lying below. The pressure to produce reaches faculty in every corner of academia. To college and university presidents, urging the importance of research is seemingly the only way, setting aside winning athletic teams, to wrest funds from legislators and donors. Occasionally a Jacques Barzun or a Page Smith will confront the research obsession. "The vast majority of what passes for research in American institutions of higher learning does not deserve the time and paper expended on it," Smith (1987, p. 52) writes. I glance at the flood of material coming across my desk that supports such a claim. The eighth annual meeting of the Semiotic Society of America held at a ski resort above Salt Lake City has papers and symposia on "Semiotics as a Critique of Derridean Poststructuralism," "The Semiotics of Intertexts," "Neglected Figures in the History of Semiotics Inquiry," "Issues in the Philosophic Foundations of Semiotics," "The Genrification of Desire: A Semiotics of Contemporary Metatheory," and on and on. From the *Chronicle of Higher Education,* I find that researchers have acquainted those at the annual meeting of the American Association for the Advancement of Science that "human facial expressions can produce mood changes as well as express them."

Students are easily impressed with academic flummery, but I think that the values and conditions I have been describing among faculty and institutions are not lost on them. The larger number of undergraduates sense the contending for power that relegates much of their instruction to a secondary position. Many sense where power lies and jockey for grades and courses that ensure their entry into fast-track occupations. If they have lost their souls, as Bloom claims, it is because the university at large has little concern for soul.

By now, I have come to believe that research is a fetish, unexplainable except as one considers other basically sexual fixations: "You show me your research and I'll show you mine." But it blights as well as informs undergraduate teaching and stands in the way of any large understanding of education itself. Perhaps power and status as well as sexuality are behind it, for it enables some part of the university and particularly those at higher administrative levels to feel they are in an enterprise as central to American displays of power as are the Pentagon and the networks and big-time sports.

One of the tangible signs of research dominance is the research park that now borders every ambitious university. The worth of these research parks can be calculated in precise terms of jobs generated and income produced, but little attention has been given to their costs and benefits for the central educational functions of a university. Nor has anyone tried to calculate the actual cost of the fetish with research as it affects every faculty member regardless of that research's economic or noneconomic worth and of its part in driving up the cost of undergraduate education. Beyond that still are those other costs, the most ominous of which is the continual piling up of research directly and indirectly expanding our insane potential for destruction, called "power."

The impact of the research fetish on undergraduate education has been ruinous. It is largely responsible for the incoherence of the curriculum as well as for its unwholesome and unattractive aspects. It is directly responsible for narrowing the conception of both teaching and learning and of debasing the general worth of both. It is directly responsible for distorting the academic reward system so that the necessary diversity of higher education—of which maintaining strong undergraduate education is a foremost concern—is badly served. And it has trivialized much learning, deadened a great deal of instruction, and distorted our conceptions of what is to be learned and how one might go about it. Among its other adverse consequences are the immense waste of young brainpower and the human and economic burden of publishing and accumulating and storing information.

The research fetish is a joint creation of faculty and university administrators. Few administrators are or remain scholars and fewer still continue with research. But that does not keep them from feeding on research, for as research must be pursued so it is also something that can be administered. One of the sinister developments in the past decade is the spread of grantsmanship to those areas of the university that had been able to maintain a clean, if parasitic, relationship to the incessant hustling for funds. Like hundreds of other institutions in the country, my university recently launched a research institute in the College of Humanities. Whatever the value of the research it produces, its effects will be to draw faculty away from teaching, from undergraduate education, and to increase, once again, that part of the educational body that has little concern or responsibility for undergraduate education. The pattern is as familiar and predictable as the creation of the administrative bureaucracy within public school education, and it exemplifies the specific and large impact administrators have on the faculty's retreat from the classroom. Unfortunately, undergraduate education is little served by the kind of grantsmanship useful to research. Undergraduate education must be broadly conceived, must get the concerted commitment of many individuals, and is not easily or at all aided by specific grants for piecemeal purposes.

The Breaking Up of Undergraduate Education

Grants serve the larger ends of undergraduate education poorly, somewhat as the conventional administrative structure of large universities gives undergraduate education little voice. Power in the university is weighted heavily by the presence of overlapping administrators and offices clustering around graduate study and research and development. Both presidents and academic vice presidents lament how their time is taken up with everything but education. The breakup in many institutions of a central College of Arts and Letters or Arts and Sciences removes the counterweight afforded by large numbers of students and faculty and some semblance of common concerns. Instead, undergraduate education is dispersed among separate college deans contending for their own disciplinary interests and knowing well where power and prestige lie. I have little hope for undergraduate education unless the undergraduate college is restored as the educational center of the university and provided with an administrative structure that can support it.

All of what I have been saying is closely related. The dominance of research that provides an escape from teaching for faculty and money and prestige for academic administrators, the presence of a large pool of not fully credentialed teachers to do the least desirable work, the outmoded administrative structure that provides little voice for undergraduate studies and little leadership for the faculty all conspire against undergraduate education. But here I will move to analogy to try to show how all these relate to an American power.

The Major Leagues and the Minor Leagues

The undergraduate college is not unlike a minor league farm team in a tank town. To the locals, it may be good enough to get a crowd out when there is nothing better on cable, but everyone, players and spectators, are aware that the real action is elsewhere. The big bucks and glory are in the major league franchises; the academic counterparts are the Harvards and Stanfords and Chicagos, the old-time champions, and a lot of new franchises, most of them state universities hell-bent on research as the way to glory. The presidents of such institutions are a cross between owners and managers; in either role the game of education is not the point—winning or appearing to be a winner is. Thus, all the practices we have been talking about obtain. Even down in the English departments, you get players saying, "We're hot now and everyone knows that. I don't think any other English department in the country can boast of the lineup of home-run hitters we've got here."

The motivation, at both institutional and personal levels, is the power that derives from running a high-flying, money-laden enterprise much in the public eye. So it is not really unusual that the late A. Bartlett Giamatti, a former English professor and president of Yale, should ascend to commissioner of a major sport. Nor is it unusual that university presidents as a group recognize clearly that maintaining professional sports within their own domain is their first duty—not only the foremost source of their personal power and glory but also an institutional obligation to all those who deserve a winning franchise.

There are weaknesses in this analogy. Professional sports are less hampered by ideals of public service than is higher education; in the sports world, it is enough of a public service to arouse and satisfy the passions of so many millions. And professional sports probably have more regard for developing the pipeline through which raw talents may be refined into superstars than universities have for the education given their average undergraduates. In fact, professional football and basketball finessed the colleges long ago by using college athletics as a cheaper way of developing talent than maintaining farm teams. Would that the sciences were as shrewd in realizing that the pool of talent for advanced research depends heavily not only on the undergraduate college but on the public schools as well.

What it comes down to is that the conduct of athletics within the major universities reveals a good deal about what undergraduate education might be. For only on that select group of athletes are the full resources of both teaching and research lavished. The teaching is both labor intensive and supported by more technology than Thomas Edison could have dreamed of. The students are highly motivated, not only by extrinsic rewards but by a corps of Ph.D. sports psychologists drawing on their latest research. The nagging pressures of education beyond the parameters of each person's specialization—slam dunking, sacking the quarterback, and contract negotiating—are removed, both by necessary tutoring and a casual attitude to the gaining of degrees. And at the end for the students and reflected back on their mentors and managers is real power, the $5 million contract and endorsements everlasting.

The wonder is that presidents and trustees have not more clearly realized how much waste is entailed in supporting a surrounding structure that contributes so little to the core enterprise. The research parks are useful, for they often provide hotel space on big-game days and more corporate entities to buy season tickets in the pricey sections. And the big-name academics are necessary to furnish the TV blurbs about the enterprises conducted on campus—heart transplants and intercontinental deconstructionist conferences—that are comparable evidence of academic power. But the rest, the numbers of professors and, for that matter, undergraduate students are far in excess of those needed to give a collegiate veneer to the game, and they take up good seats that might better be sold to alumni.

Conclusion

Well, to come back to Bloom, he's missed most of this badly, probably because Chicago, for inexplicable reasons unless you count consistent losing as explicable, gave up big-time athletics even before his time. Still, he might have realized that rock and roll, which he abuses, is more central to modern life, even in south Chicago, than whatever it is he purports to teach. You want power, man? Turn it up. Move 'em out.

I have extended these reflections in *The Aims of College Teaching* (1983). The central part of that book is animated by the feeling I share with John Seeley when he writes: "Western civilization lies all but dead under its own learned knife" (p. 71). What I fear is knowledge grown into a dogmatic theology in which its pursuit is the only unquestioned virtue. The graduate schools are its ecclesiastical centers and graduate professors its high priests. And like the papal church of the past, it goes its way ostensibly arguing its spirituality but being shaped and directed by a desire for materialistic power.

In this context, I find Bloom's (1987) book, with its concern for the souls of students and its vision confined to "the kind of young persons who populate the twenty or thirty best universities" (p. 22), a monastic exercise defending established dogma and established power. I am interested in the larger world where the most successful large democratic state the world has known seems to be letting the desire for power cause the neglect of the education of the majority of citizens—on whom the health of that democracy depends. I may agree with Bloom with respect to the care of the soul here, but it is the soul of the university rather than of the students that gives me most concern. For if the university still has a soul, it must be in undergraduate education, which still can provide a place for students and faculty to resist some of the seduction of power.

References

Adams, H. *The Education of Henry Adams*. (E. Samuels, ed.) Boston: Houghton Mifflin, 1974. (Originally published 1918.)
Bloom, A. *The Closing of the American Mind*. New York: Simon & Schuster, 1987.
Eble, K. E. *The Aims of College Teaching*. San Francisco: Jossey-Bass, 1983.
Eble, K. E. *The Craft of Teaching: A Guide to Mastering the Professor's Art*. (2nd ed.) San Francisco: Jossey-Bass, 1988.
Franklin, P., Laurence, D., and Denham, R. "When Solutions Become Problems: Taking a Stand on Part-Time Employment." *Academe*, May–June 1988, pp. 15–19.
Seeley, J. "The University as Slaughterhouse." In *The Great Ideas Today 1969*. New York: Praeger, 1969.
Smith, P. "To Communicate Truth: How Research Corrupts Teaching." *Whole Earth Review*, Summer 1987, p. 52.

Kenneth E. Eble was professor of English and University Professor, University of Utah. He was the author of The Craft of Teaching: A Guide to Mastering the Professor's Art *(Jossey-Bass, 1988) and numerous other books.*

College ranking scales, projects for image enhancement, and similar paraphernalia that preoccupy today's university administrators detract from the main business of undergraduate teaching and liberal education.

The Art of Deliberalizing: A Handbook for the True Professional

Wayne C. Booth

> Another way in which teaching may seem to be losing its point for faculty and students is through the loss of simple pleasures in learning. The increased emphasis upon scholarship, the support of research, the tendency to make professional training the central purpose of every discipline, have brought more satisfaction to professors than to undergraduate students. I am not talking here just about the major university centers.... I am talking about broader effects of the professional emphasis.
> —Eble, 1972.

I must confess that when Carol Schneider first phoned to ask me to give this speech I was very reluctant indeed. "Look, Carol," I said, "Let's face it. I don't have anything brand new to say about liberal education. Or the role of the college. Or the teacher's vocation. Or the development of major fields. I've squandered it all in past books and speeches, and ..."

"But, Wayne," she interrupted, "How many listeners will expect to hear anything new in a keynote speech?"

There was a long silence.

This chapter (copyright 1990 by Wayne C. Booth) was the keynote address at the seventy-sixth annual meeting of the Association of American Colleges, January 10-13, 1990, in San Francisco. Reprints are available for $5 each from the Publications Desk, Association of American Colleges, 1818 R Street, N.W., Washington, D.C. 20009. Epigraph added by the editor of this volume.

"And so, why not . . ." she said, "Why not just come along and feed us the old stuff to show how somebody of advanced years hangs in . . ."

This time I interrupted. "Hold on," I said. "That advanced years stuff is not the road to my heart. How much will you pay?"

"We have a flat rate of ten dollars an hour."

"Ten dollars an hour!" I said. "Wait just a darn minute. That's not enough to drag an elderly gentleman from his lair into earthquake-threatened territory to say what he's already said before."

"Why isn't it enough?" she snapped. "It's better than the majority of beginning teachers average today: the part-timers, ABDs, and TAs who staff our required general-education courses. A recent study shows that those on 'half-time' schedules work an average of thirty to forty hours a week and are paid roughly a thousand bucks a course. You can work that hourly wage out for yourself. Do you honestly think that giving a keynote speech is worth more than teaching a freshman class?"

There was another even longer silence.

"Do you think"—Carol is known for relentless pursuit of a point once she has an adversary on the ropes—"Do you honestly think that a forty-minute hour giving a keynote speech is worth more than a fifty-minute hour giving one's best to reading freshmen papers?"

She had me there, and she knew she had me. I argued for a while, though, pointing out that most people in the world apparently *do* rank freshman teaching not only lower than giving keynote speeches, but actually as the lowest on the so-called higher education totem pole. "So why," I went on, "Why shouldn't we go along with this established hierarchy?"

But she kept at me, and when she finally raised the pay to twenty dollars for forty minutes—that's fifty cents a minute, which she figures is the average pay of beginning full-timers—I accepted.

I'll spare you the details of how she talked me into the present title, which I can't claim even now to understand. But with a title like that, as the time drew closer—and with nothing to say—I naturally felt more and more desperate. As late as yesterday afternoon, I was about to phone her and say, "Sorry, I've had a terrible attack of diverticulitis," when I received a fat express mail package, opened it in a mood of desperation, and within ten minutes knew that I had been rescued. It turned out to be a long personal letter, accompanying a committee report, written by my lifetime friend Sophonisba Q. Smith, Dean of the Humanities Division at Upwardly Mobile Research College, which many of you will know under its former name, UM College.

Now Sophie Smith has been dean of Upwardly Mobile for five years, throughout the period of its meteoric rise on all the national reputation scales. Many of you probably saw just this week in the *Chronicle* that UMRC, now affectionately referred to locally as "Humwreck"—some pronounce it "Yoomwreck"—UMRC has now risen from a low point somewhere far off the chart even of mere liberal arts colleges to a ranking as #36 in CRAS's monthly ranking of research colleges.

I can see by the look on some of your faces that you may not yet know about CRAS. You will. These things move fast, and you should know that the College Ranking Ascent Scale (CRAS) is one of the most powerful tools for educational improvement that this nation has ever developed. Any dean, any provost, any chair at any of the top fifty-four colleges or any of the top thirty-seven *research* colleges now can point monthly to precise, computerized evidence of just what's been achieved national-reputation-wise during the preceding month.

As I said, Yoomwreck has at last broken into the magic circle of the top thirty-seven research colleges. Incidentally, I'm sure nobody here will confuse the CRAS list with the list of fifty-eight research universities that belong to the Association of American Universities (AAU). That list is what the research colleges on the CRAS scale aspire to *join,* someday in the far future. The CRAS list is the list that colleges join when they succeed in earning national acclaim not as mere colleges but as *research* colleges.

Is that distinction among the three lists clear? As an official of the National Collegiate Athletic Association said just yesterday, "Things can get pretty unfair when judges get their categories of institutions confused."

It was clear to me, in reading Dean Smith's account of how Yoomwreck had climbed from the bottom list to the middle list, that it was just what this convention needed to hear about.

First, though, I have to share one little worry. I've had time to read only once through Dean Smith's rather long-winded mailing—speed-reading at that—just before I caught my plane, and I approach reading it here with some anxiety for fear I'd make some of you anxious. It reveals Yoomwreck so far ahead of what most of us even imagined as possibilities for improvement that you may want to leave the hall even as I speak to go to your fax machines and alert people back home to get cracking in the new direction. Even as you sit here it's possible that your college is slipping a notch when it could be—if you were on the job—climbing. So feel free to leave at any point; I'll know how to interpret your departure.

I do have another small anxiety. I'm not sure that Dean Smith would agree to my revealing Yoomwreck's secrets. Could leaking them to you dull Yoomwreck's competitive edge? After all, there are only thirty-seven places. I am reassured, though, by Dean Smith's postscript, in which she tells me that Yoomwreck is by no means resting on its laurels. She says that it fully expects to be in the lower thirties by late spring, and they're even thinking of a name and category change from Upwardly Mobile Research College to Upwardly Mobile University, hoping someday to rival Rutgers and SUNY-Buffalo's recent rise to membership in the Association of American Universities. As AAU President Robert M. Rosenzweig said in explaining SUNY-Buffalo's elevation: "All of the data we had on the question of quality showed that the university had come a long way in the past decade, and was up at the top of the public institutions that were not yet members of AAU."

Perhaps some of you are impatient by now—ten minutes along—for the handbook promised in my title. Well, you should have figured out that the handbook never got written. In its place you have only what Dean Smith has sent. In my view, there is no "art of deliberalizing." Deliberalizing doesn't require an art; it just happens automatically. All the art lies in *liberalizing* in such a way as to ensure a rise in the CRAS scale. Who would want a handbook of *deliberalizing*? Nobody. So just be patient, as I read her letter and then her committee report.

She begins:

I should confess right away that I was not at first sold on President Earl Y. Rising's first statement of his plan. It seemed to me that Early, as we now call him, talked too freely and optimistically about his hopes for change. And I must confess that, already then in my third year as dean, I was in a rather dry, pessimistic period. I'd been struggling—blindly and halfheartedly, as I now see it—to obtain higher salaries for all my faculty and a reduced teaching load for those who taught required freshmen courses and any required courses in major fields, especially those that included a lot of writing.

The administration of President Doldrum, Rising's predecessor, had seen no point in rewarding teachers who, as Doldrum put it, "were already fully committed to staying at UMC anyway, and couldn't get jobs elsewhere if they tried." So I'd been getting nowhere with him, and I was beginning to believe that we would never get anywhere, that Upwardly Mobile College would forever remain off everybody's charts. So when President Rising arrived, my hopes rose. He had impressed us all in preliminary interviews with his promises to raise salaries and improve our image, or, in his language, "to put UMC on the map of American higher education."

But, as I said, my hopes were somewhat dimmed when I received his first memo, addressed to all our deans. As a lifetime teacher of English, I have to admit that I found his prose style a bit off-putting—perhaps not quite so disturbing as the prose of another high-ranking president I could name, but still full of clumsy redundancies and solecisms. The substance also disturbed me.

Then Sophie goes on to quote Rising's first memo:

"To: All Deans at UMC
From: President E. Y. Rising
Subject: Our Image

"As will be remembered by those of you who attended the interview before I was chosen, a major prime emphasis of my administration will be to improve the image, standing, and reputation of UMC. You should not need to be told that such a goal will require the absolutely devoted application, drive, and energy of every administrator. Let's face it: some difficult, painful decisions face us all in the troubled days that lie ahead, which are, after all, our future.

"Our first step must be actually **two** steps. First, it will be imperative to have prepared by every institutional unit [he meant 'department'] a list, however short, of just which current activities and programs can be given effective image enhancement with respect to any one of our possible constituencies. The second step is like unto the first: we must request of every employee unit . . . (Dean Smith interpolates in handwriting in the margin, *I still bridle at his use of the term 'employee unit' for faculty member*) a twofold memo delineating first precisely what he or she now does that if properly packaged could yield image enhancement, and secondly what new or different form of activity could, again assuming proper packaging, yield a better image-to-product ratio-scale.

"Today is being appointed by my office a vice president for image enhancement, and established a new division—the Program for Image Enhancement, or PIE. **Our** goal is to join the by-now universal national Program for Image Enhancement—what you've been observing in the national news recently—and to increase our share of the national PIE. **Your** goal—the goal of each and every dean, chair, and employee unit—is to increase his or her share of the **local** image PIE."

As I, Wayne Booth, think about this now for the first time, it does strike me that the national PIE *is* getting bigger all the time.

As I said (continuing now with Sophonisba's letter), my heart was not lifted up by this memo. It was not that I objected so much to the professed goal of PIE but that I knew how the teachers in my division would respond. I could picture the two professors of Latin and the one professor of Greek simply snorting, if they didn't start shaking in their boots. The three professors of German, the one professor of biblical history—what could they say in response to such a memo? I did in fact later receive angry memos such as the one from an irate professor who said, "After all, it is not our job to stand to one side of the ladder of success and goose our students as they climb."

Indeed, as I ran over in my mind what I considered the real virtues of my division, I could think of only one likely image-builder, one small program that might yield a piece of the PIE: Professor Copper's computer program for automatic spotting and correcting of grammatical errors. Copper calls it "PURGE": "Purify Your Grammar and English." PURGE had already been featured on our local television as a product that was selling like . . . well, like computer software, and I knew that Rising would be pleased to hear about it.

But what could I, or any of the other teachers, say about our programs? For example, our really quite decent required general-ed courses in literature and composition—that is to say, our new attempt to get some coherence, some sense of community, and real inquiry into our major fields? Our students were learning to read, write, think, and speak responsibly. They were, we felt, becoming intellectually empowered as independent inquirers. They were taught by hard-working teachers who required lots of writing and who met regularly together to discuss how to do a better job. New teachers received careful orientation in the fall and throughout the first two or three years. Obviously there was nothing to contribute to PIE in any of that. What image could it produce? Nothing. Niente. Zilch.

Still, I pulled myself together, Wayne, and passed along instructions to the faculty and set about preparing my own memo asking them to respond to the PIE request. The only PIE item that they surprised me with in response was the description of a new multi-media course in American history, to be taught by Professor Hyperstat, called AMHISTPRIME. The fact is that Hyperstat's plan saved—well, to put it inelegantly to an old friend—Hyperstat saved my butt. Though everything else in my division looked hopeless, I now had something for Rising.

It is true that the first report of AMHISTPRIME had a lot of bugs in it, and my lukewarm forwarding memo didn't quite sell it to Rising. I'll spare you the details now of how, over some months, I gradually became more enthusiastic as we sharpened things up and sold Rising on the idea. I give here only a copy of excerpts from part of our final plan, now in place, thanks to a widely publicized grant from the Reynolds Tobacco Company.

Note, Wayne (she adds), that this is not my report, only the plan. I'm sorry to go on so long, but if you're to understand our report all this background is essential.

"To: Department of History, UMC
From: Dean Sophonisba Smith
Subject: Planning for PIE

"To realize the goals of President Rising in improving our national PIE level, it has been agreed that the history department, in addition to improving the ratio of pages published to line positions, will develop as our central American history undergraduate major a new program that will be called AMHISTPRIME. This program consists of five steps:

"1. The history department will develop for the first time a graduate Ph.D. program in American history, leading to M.A. and Ph.D. degrees. As everyone knows, the mere existence of a Ph.D. program, good or bad, ensures at least a two-point rise on the CRAS waiting list. What's more, AMHISTPRIME as a major for B.A.s will require a fresh supply of teaching assistants, and how can you get enough of those without a Ph.D. program?

"2. Graduate students will be chosen on the basis of both previous academic achievement and their ability to act in front of a television camera.

"3. All lecture sections will be videotapes of historical events as dramatized by those skilled teaching assistants, Professor Hyperstat serving as director and producer of the videotapes—which will be made nationally available at a nominal charge to all local stations and networks.

"4. In place of the traditional discussion sections and essay assignments for undergrads in AMHISTPRIME, the TAs—from now on to be called DAs (for 'dramatization actualizers')—will produce dramatic performances and videotapes based on whatever historical events have been chosen as the center of that week's study. These videotapes will be marketed under the names of the senior professors, and the DAs will also be on the list, and the citation will count toward promotion as publications."

Here, I'm afraid I have to skip the rest of the history plan. Sophie goes on to describe similar imaginative programs in other departments—one in literature ("Live Lit"), one in philosophy ("The Visible Platonist: Ideas in Action"), and so on.

Meanwhile (her letter continues), the social sciences were developing similar ideas: a videotape portraying Marxist and Weberian protagonists in bloody combat, film files with original docudramas of every known culture. In short, our students were no longer faced with outmoded demands that they read tough, impenetrable prose by major figures; ideas were now given life, and that life, since it was intelligible to the broader public in simple terms, was already producing better PIE.

The sciences, too, had developed programs for enlivening their instruction and reducing its costs. Though they already had a leaping head start in the matter of PIE—since most of what they do is, after all, tangible or visible already—they soon learned how to increase their PIE points by reducing the teaching loads of the stars even further and encouraging the stars instead to spend more time ensuring the proper public attention to their work. Whereas in the past the mean lead time between the conception of a new scientific possibility and the milking of PIE credit from the idea had been seven years, the chairman of physics proudly announced that his top three researchers had reduced that time to three days. One specialist in chaos theory even managed to get publicity for his idea before he had it. Needless to say, some of his more envious colleagues accused him of going too far. But President Rising has appointed a committee to look into further possibilities in that direction.

So much for curriculum and my conversion to PIE. It soon became evident that with the help of AMHISTPRIME and the other sellable courses, UMC's PIE program was now earning a gratifyingly larger share of the national PIE.

But what of the rest of Rising's program? We all knew the curriculum could never do it alone. How have we managed to climb from nowhere to #36? President Rising here again showed his almost incredible intuitive sense of what will grab America's attention.

I remember one luncheon with all deans and vice presidents when Rising laid out his plan.

"Well folks," he said, "how are we doin'?"

We cheered.

"So what do you think are the next steps?" He stared around the table at twenty silent faces, all eyes lowered.

"The next step," he went on, "is obviously to construct a list of what innovations besides curriculum will create image. Now what's first on such a list?"

More silence.

He lost his cool. "Why must I provide all the ideas?" he snarled.

But immediately he was smiling again into the silence. Finally, the dean of physical sciences said, almost sotto voce, "Buy some Nobel prize winners?"

President Rising looked appalled. "You think that a college in UMC's position could buy a Nobel laureate? Upwardly mobile research universities like Pseud U can do that, but we can't. At least not yet. Think again."

More silence.

*Finally, I said, "Less **expensive** prizes, less **important** stars?"*

"You've got it!" Rising almost shouted. "I want a list from every one of you of purchasable stars by next Monday, with estimates of the price. Understood?"

We all nodded, mute.

He himself broke the silence this time.

"I know what you're all thinking. You're wondering where—if my recent report on our budget cuts and the costs of the new Department of Computerized Advertising is accurate—the money will come from, even for cheap stars. Isn't the answer obvious? The biggest item in our budget is instruction; the instructional budget is our obvious source. You all know as well as I do that there are a lot more unemployed Ph.D.s out there than we've ever reached, so let's reach them. Our line positions now cost an average of $40,000 a year. I don't have to tell you that we can get up to eight half-timers—that's four full teaching loads—for $40,000. Until further notice, we're shutting down all line positions. Every retirement, death, or other departure from any department will open two non-line FTEs for that department. The other half, the sheer savings, will go to my PIE fund for hiring those stars that you, if you're smart, will start locating nationally and internationally today. Got it?"

You may feel some relief, as I did, when I saw that there was only one more paragraph in Sophie's personal letter.

It read, Well, that's enough of how I got sold on the program. Rising then made me chair of the Committee on PIE, or COPIE, and I enclose a copy of our report. I have not talked with him yet about it, but the provost met me in the hall yesterday and said that Rising is very pleased. The provost thinks we're on our way to carrying out most of our suggestions.

"To: President Rising

From: Committee on PIE, Sophonisba Q. Smith, Chair

"We want to express our gratitude to President Rising for what he has done for us and for what we hope will soon be known nationally as 'UMRC'. The rapidity with which our new curriculum has been developed and our recent successes in hiring four nationally luminous non-teachers for only $125,000 each—and that against competition from Texas and California—has preempted much of what our report would have had to deal with. In our view the remaining elements in the PIE program probably should include the following:

"1. To continue our present trend toward a more luminous faculty, we strongly recommend that no further significant raises be given except in response to outside offers. Too many of our faculty members are still unknown except locally. One of our committee members did argue for a while that the way to build a strong faculty is to find nonluminous people who are really gifted and reward them so handsomely that they don't feel any need to seek outside offers. But we soon convinced Oldheimer that the only sure way to judge the quality of one's colleagues is by their outside image.

"2. Organize a series of conferences that will bring to campus prominent thinkers who will meet with faculty members only, in closed sessions, uncluttered by the presence of uninformed students: conferences on such PIE-rich topics as 'The Liberal Education of the Future,' 'The Research College of the Year 2000,' and so on. Then we can publish conference reports that will redound to our credit.

"3. *Continue to honor faculty members for teaching.* One member of the committee has argued that we should cancel our teaching prizes, thus saving the $4,000 a year that they cost us—almost enough to hire one half-timer for a full year. But the majority—this may surprise you—argued that image-wise it is important to retain those prizes. UMC, or if we become UMRC, should continue to proclaim to the world that we do honor teaching as much as we ever did, maybe more. Some of our more recent moves have led some students, and some parents of students, and even some people in the general public—**even some faculty members**—to question whether we're neglecting liberal education in the service of other goals. In all that we do, we should remember that there is still a nationwide anxiety about the preservation of devoted teaching of the liberal arts. Nothing will scotch rumors of our betraying those arts more effectively than talking loud and clear and often about our devotion to teaching the liberal arts.

"4. *Set up a committee whose task is to find out the next national trend and recommend ways of joining it.* (Sophie interrupts the report here to explain that The Trend Committee was appointed and that its first report revolutionized the major fields that had not already followed AMHIST-PRIME's lead in video production. They recommended, and Yoomwreck implemented, a set of majors based on the cultural literacy movement but concentrating on those cultural literacy terms that need to be used by advanced workers in each field. For example, the major in Cultural Literacy and Literary Criticism, CLLC, covers all the terms now found in literary journals. *Nothing,* she adds, *has brought us more PIE than our graduates' recent performance on national vocabulary tests.*)

"5. *Cut our remaining ties with the public schools.* Everybody knows that the schools are at the bottom of the image pile, and in fact they taint everything they touch. UMC's long history of preparing teachers committed to liberal education is now one big liability. The energy and money we've been spending in the effort to give prospective teachers a liberal education could now go into the PIE fund, perhaps earmarked for a new named professorship in educational research. Or we could establish a Bennett-Hirsch fund for more and more studies of just what bits of information our students lack. We might then harvest some of the PIE that is flung nationally when such studies are released."

Well, I'm afraid the committee report continues for many more pages, and my time is almost up. The report covers many further possibilities that any college might well consider if it becomes seriously concerned about its own PIE. It recommends, for example, a multimillion-dollar campaign to finance a new building—state of the art—devoted to the technologies of information transfer. It recommends a vast increase in programs specifically financed by particular businesses for training students in the skills those businesses need. It recommends that all writing instruction be done by computer and closed-circuit television. It recommends abandoning the autumn faculty retreat on the aims of education because, after all, who cares about that? It reports on a recent issue of *People* magazine in which Yoomwreck's interdisciplinary program is celebrated: the videodramatization of the great ideas in each discipline—known as GREED.

I must cut off Dean Smith's letter, however, and limp to my anticlimax. Personally, I, Wayne Booth, wish I could wholeheartedly buy all of Yoomwreck's imaginative PIE, but I confess that a few of the suggestions seem to go a bit too far. On the other hand, it would be folly, wouldn't it, to reject the Smith/Rising Upwardly Mobile plan in toto? Who among us—deans, provosts, presidents, chancellors, vice chancellors, professors, keynote speakers—could hope to continue in our present comfortable positions at colleges with their present CRAS and AAU standing and continue to be sent to conferences in San Francisco at a hotel like this if we decided to . . . well, ah, how should we put this? Who among us could *afford* to stop whatever we're doing about PIE now, whether at Yoomwreck or at places like the University of Chicago, and return to a total commitment to—dare I use that old term—"liberal education?"

Postscript (March 1, 1990)

A colleague at Santa Cruz asked me, after reading this transcript, why I let myself sound as if I were above the battle—why I seemed to exempt myself and my "research university" from the satire. "Why talk as if *you and your kind* were untainted by the evils of PIE? There you are, already an 'established' figure at an 'established' university—one of the 'cheap stars' in Rising's terms. What right have you to raise questions about the efforts of those who would like to improve their lot?"

There is only one possible answer to that kind of envious reading of my humble effort: At the University of Chicago we *are* above the battle. I know that some students of envy claim that "everyone feels some envy," especially "in those domains of life that matter the most for your own view of yourself" (Dr. Peter Salovey of Yale University, quoted in "Envy Seen as Sensitive Barometer," *New York Times,* 27 Feb. 1990, C1). But they must be wrong, because after years of effort we have all purged ourselves of every last vestige of interest in PIE. We have thus eliminated every office and fired every employee formerly charged with image enhancement; we no longer even *look* at the various reports of national institutional standings. I never hear any conversation among faculty members about why our English department, for example, is always listed lower than Harvard's and Yale's, and *much too often* lower even than *far inferior places* like Princeton, Berkeley, Virginia, Johns Hopkins, Columbia, Cornell, and others I could name if I paid any attention to such matters. If I may take myself as an example, I have for some years now been entirely freed of any remnant of worry about image. I didn't even notice, for example, that a recent survey of today's important literary critics, published in a journal I will not name, did not *have the courtesy* to mention my work. With my mind and heart entirely devoted to liberal education, how could I stoop to wondering why a certain unnamed university in the East has *never even once* invited me to lecture there?

So you see, this little talk just doesn't apply to us at Chicago; it applies only to those institutions who are above us or below us in the national rankings.

Reference

Eble, K. E. *Professors as Teachers.* San Francisco: Jossey-Bass, 1972.

Wayne C. Booth is George M. Pullman Distinguished Service Professor at the University of Chicago.

Education in a democratic society must include education about, by, and for minorities.

The Transforming of the American Mind

Henry Louis Gates, Jr.

> Like many things that catch the headlines and some things which take up the attention of faculty members, the increased visibility of blacks, Chicanos, Indians, and the poor within higher education is disproportionate to the actual increase in their numbers. . . . Few colleges can escape recognition of the needs of these individuals who give more scope to the term *student.*
> —Eble, 1972.

When I'm asked to talk about the opening of the American mind, or the decentering of the humanities, or the new multiculturalism—or any number of such putative developments—I have to say my reaction is pretty much the same as Mahatma Gandhi's when they asked him what he thought about Western civilization. He said he thought it would be a good idea. My sentiments exactly.

This decade has, to be sure, witnessed an interesting coupling of trends. On the one hand, we've seen calls from on high to reclaim a legacy, to fend off the barbarians at the gates, and to return to some prelapsarian state of grace. On the other hand (or is it the same hand?), we've seen a disturbing recrudescence of campus racism sweeping the nation. Many of you will have seen lead articles about this in issues of the *Chronicle of Higher Education,* but the topic has been in the news for quite some time. For people who agitated in the civil rights era and saw real gains in the

---

This chapter was presented as the Literature Lecture at the University of Texas at El Paso on March 8th, 1990. The epigraph was added by the editor.

college curriculum in the 1970s, the new conservatism seems to have succeeded their own efforts rather as the Redemption politicians followed the Reconstruction, threatening to undo what progress had been made.

One thing is clear. Education in a democratic society (or one that aspires to that ideal) has particular burdens placed on it. Few theorists of American education, in this century or the preceding one, separated pedagogy from the needs of citizenship. The usual term here is often given a sinister intonation: social reproduction. . . . Yet this country has always had an evolutionary view of what reproduction entails. We've never been content with mere replication; we've sought improvement. We want our kids to be better than we are.

So it is discouraging, even painful to look at our colleges, bastions of liberal education, and find that people are now beginning to talk—and with justice, it seems—about the "new racism." I don't want to offer a simple diagnosis, but perhaps the phenomenon isn't completely unconnected to larger political trends. It's been pointed out that today's freshmen were ten years old when the Reagan era began; presumably the public discourse of the eighties may have something to do with the forming of these students' political sensibilities.

But whatever the causes, the climate on campus has been worsening: According to one monitoring group ("Blacks and Whites on the Campuses," 1990), racial incidents have been reported at over 175 colleges since the 1986–87 school year. And that's just counting the cases that made the papers.

At the same time, there has been, since 1977, a marked decline in overall black enrollment in colleges (Press, 1986). The evidence suggests that the decline is connected to a slipping economic situation and to cuts in available federal aid. In the decade since 1977, federal grants and scholarships have fallen 62 percent, and that, of course, disproportionately affects minority students. Almost half of all black children (46.7 percent) live below the poverty line, according to the Congressional Research Service. Indeed, if you look at students at traditionally black colleges, you find that 42 percent of them come from families with incomes below the poverty line; a third of these students come from families with a total family income of less than $6,000 a year. So when it comes to larger economic trends, blacks are like the canaries in the coal mine: the first to go when things are going wrong.

But there's an even bigger problem than getting these students, and that's keeping them. The attrition rate is depressing. At the University of California, Berkeley, one in four black students will graduate. According to the National Center of Education Statistics (Marquand, 1988) only 31 percent of freshmen blacks in 1980 had graduated by 1986. And while financial pressures explain some of this attrition they don't explain all of it.

Down the educational pike, things get worse. Just 2.3 percent of our full-time college professors are black, and the number is said to be decreasing. In 1986, only 820 of the 32,000 Ph.D.'s awarded went to blacks; less than half of that 820 plan a college career (that's 1 percent of our new Ph.D.s).

In short, it's a bad situation. But it's not a conspiracy; nobody wants it to be the way it is. In general, our colleges really are devoted to diversity, and administrators are genuinely upset when they fail to incorporate diversity among their students and faculty. I said before that the peculiar charge of our education system is the shaping of a democratic polity. It's a reflection of the public consensus on this matter that one of the few bipartisan issues in the last presidential campaign had to do with equitable access to higher education. Pollsters on both sides found that this was an issue that made the American heart skip a beat. Equal opportunity in education is an idea with broad appeal in this country. And that has something to do with what education means to us. So one thing I want to bring out is that the schools are a site where real contradictions and ambivalences are played out.

I would like to talk today about institutions for higher learning in terms of the larger objectives of what we call a liberal education. As unfashionable as it is among many of my fellow theorists, I do believe in the humanities, broadly conceived. But it's that breadth of conception I want to address. We hear the complaints. Allan Bloom (1987), for example, laments that "just at the moment when everyone else has become a 'person', blacks have become blacks" (p. 92). (Needless to say, underlying this view is the idea that "everyone else" can become a person precisely when the category *person* comes to be defined in contradistinction to black.) Many thoughtful educators are dismayed, even bewildered, when minority students—at Berkeley or Stanford or Texas or Oberlin, the sentiment's widespread—say that they feel like visitors, like guests, like foreign or colonized citizens in relation to a traditional canon that fails to represent their cultural identities. I'm not interested in simply endorsing their sentiment. It's not a reasoned argument, this reaction, but it is a playing out—a logical extension—of an ideology resident in the traditional rhetoric about Western civilization. And I want to consider it in that light.

Cultural Geneticism

Once upon a time, there was a race of men who could claim all of knowledge as their purview. Someone like Francis Bacon really did try to organize all of knowledge into a single capacious but coherent structure. And even into the nineteenth century the creed of universal knowledge—*mathesis universalis*—still reigned. There's a wonderful piece of nineteenth-century student doggerel about Jowett, the Victorian classicist and master of Balliol College, Oxford, which rather sums up the philosophy (McFarland, 1987):

> Here stand I, my name is Jowett,
>   If there's knowledge, then I know it;
> I am the master of this college,
>   What I know not, is not knowledge.

But how does something get to count as knowledge? Intellectuals, Gramsci (1971) famously observes, can be defined as experts in legitimation, and the academy today is an institution of legitimation—establishing what counts as knowledge, what counts as culture. In the most spirited attacks on the movement toward multiculturalism in the academy today, there's a whiff of the old doggerel: We are the masters of this college/What we know not, is not knowledge. In the wake of Bacon's epistemic megalomania, there has been a contrary movement, a constriction of what counts as even worth knowing. We've got our culture, what more do we need? Besides, there was Heidegger (1958) on stage right, assuring us that "philosophy speaks Greek." And beyond the cartography of Western culture? A cryptic warning: Here Be Monsters.

"I got mine"—the rhetoric of liberal education remains suffused with the imagery of possession, patrimony, legacy, lineage, inheritance; call it cultural geneticism (in the broadest sense of that term). At the same moment, the rhetoric of possession and lineage subsists on and perpetuates a division: between us and them, we the heirs of our tradition, and you, the Others, whose difference defines our identity. (In the French colonies, in Africa and the Caribbean, a classroom of African students would dutifully read from their textbook, "Our ancestors, the Gauls . . ." Well, you could see that wasn't going to last.)

What happens, though, if you buy into that rhetoric—if you accept its terms and presuppositions about cultural geneticism? Then you will say, Yes, I am Other, and if the aim of education is to reinforce an individual's rightful cultural legacy, then I don't belong here—I am a guest at someone else's banquet. Foucault (1977) called this kind of contestation that of "reverse discourse": It remains entrapped within the presuppositions of the discourse it means to oppose, enacting a conflict internal to that "master discourse." But when the terms of argument have already been defined, it may look like the only form of contestation possible.

One of the most eloquent reflections on this sense of entrapment is James Baldwin's (1955), where the rhetoric of dispossession turns to that of cultural reappropriation:

> I know, in any case, that the most crucial time in my own development came when I was forced to recognize that I was a kind of bastard of the West; when I followed the line of my past I did not find myself in Europe but in Africa. And this meant that in some subtle way, in a really profound way, I brought to Shakespeare, Bach, Rembrandt, to the stones

of Paris, to the cathedral at Chartres, and to the Empire State Building, a special attitude. These were not really my creations, they did not contain my history; I might search in them in vain forever for any reflection of myself. I was an interloper; this was not my heritage. At the same time, I had no other heritage which I could possibly hope to use—I had certainly been unfitted for the jungle or the tribe. I would have to appropriate these white centuries, I would have to make them mine—I would have to accept my special attitude, my special place in this scheme—otherwise I would have no place in any scheme [pp. 6-7].

This terror of having no place in any scheme contrasts oddly with the more familiar modernist anxiety of the Western writer, the anxiety that one fits into a scheme all too easily, all too well.

If Richard Wright's (1956) comments are characteristically blunter, they are no less anxious: "I'm black. I'm a man of the West. . . . I see and understand the non- or anti-Western point of view" (p. 349). But, Wright confesses, "when I look out upon the vast stretches of this earth inhabited by brown, black, and yellow men, . . . my reactions and attitudes are those of the West" (p. 349). Wright never had clearer insight into himself, but his ambivalent relation to both the Western and non-Western cultures was satisfactorily resolved. So long as we retain a vocabulary of heritage and inheritance in defining our putative national cultures, it cannot be resolved.

The argument has been made that cultural nationalism has been a constitutive aspect of Western education. As humanists, our challenge today is simply to learn to live without it. Indeed, it saddens me that there should be any perceived conflict between the ideal of humanistic learning and what I think of as the truly human, and humane, version of the humanities, one that sees the West not as some mythical, integrative Whole, but as a part of a still larger whole. In the resonant words of W.E.B. Du Bois (1965), "I sit with Shakespeare, and he winces not" (p. 284).

I believe we can change the terms of argument; I believe we can rethink the role of a liberal education without the conceptual residue of cultural nationalism or geneticism. I believe it because I think many scholars have already begun to do so.

Broadening Our Educational Vistas

Some people have begun to realize that broadening our educational vistas is not only sweet but useful. As most of you will know, a panel of United States governors recently concluded that America's economic and cultural dominance has been endangered by our vast ignorance of the languages and cultures of other nations. In a report made public on February 25, 1990, the National Governors Association argued for broad changes in the way we teach foreign languages and basic geography. Among the report's more startling findings are the following:

- A recent Gallup poll revealed that young American adults know less about geography than their peers in six developed countries.
- One in seven American adults cannot locate the United States on a world map.
- Twenty-five percent of a sample of high school seniors in Dallas, Texas, did not know that Mexico was the country bordering the U.S. to the south.
- Only twenty percent of American high school graduates receive more than two years' instruction in a foreign language.

In response to this report, Ernest L. Boyer, the president of the Carnegie Foundation for the Advancement of Teaching, remarked that "a curriculum with international perspective" is "critically important to the future of our nation."

Well, Americans know so little about world history and culture in part because high school and college core curricula in this country center on European and American societies, with America represented as the logical conclusion or summary of civilization since the Greeks, in the same way that Christians believe that Christ is the culmination of the Old Testament prophecies. Our ignorance of physical geography is a symptom of a much broader ignorance of the world's cultural geography. Since the trivium and quadrivium of the Latin Middle Ages, "the humanities" have not meant the best that has been thought by all human beings; rather, "the humanities" has meant the best that has been thought by white males in the Greco-Roman, Judeo-Christian traditions. A tyrannical pun obtains between the words *humanity*, on the one hand, and the *humanities*, on the other.

As I tried to show in a 1989 essay in the *New York Times* book review section, we need to reform our entire notion of core curricula and account for the comparable eloquence of the African, the Asian, the Latin American, and the Middle Eastern traditions in order to prepare our students for their roles in the twenty-first century as citizens of a world culture, educated through a truly human notion of the humanities.

Fragmenting Versus Decentering the Humanities

Now, I talked earlier about the long-dead ideal of universal knowledge. Today, you look back to C. P. Snow's complaint about the gulf between the "two cultures," and you think, two? Keep counting, C. P. The familiar buzzwords that apply here are the "fragmentation of humanistic knowledge." And there are people who think that the decentering of the humanities that I advocate will just make a bad situation worse: bring on the ivory towers of Babel. So I want to say a few words about this.

There are, certainly, different kinds of fragmentation. One kind of fragmentation is just the inevitable result of the knowledge explosion; specialized fields produce specialized knowledge, and there's too much to keep up with. But there's another kind of fragmentation that does deserve scrutiny: the kind that makes knowledge produced in one discipline inaccessible to scholars in another discipline, even when that knowledge would be useful for them in solving their problems. And here what I call the decentering of the humanities can help us rethink some of the ways in which traditional subjects are constituted and will allow us a critical purchase helpful in cultural studies generally. Indeed, far from being inimical to traditional Western scholarship, humanistic scholarship in Asian and African cultures can be mutually enriching to it, to the humanities in general. And that's as you'd expect, since the study of the humanities is the study of the possibilities of human life in culture. It thrives on diversity. And when you get down to cases, it's hard to deny that what you could call the new scholarship has invigorated the traditional disciplines. Historians of black America have pioneered work in oral history that's had a significant effect on the way nineteenth-century social history is done. Think of the upheavals in Homeric scholarship from Milman Parry's (1987) work on those Yugoslavian bards—or the advances in understanding the epic from Jack Goody's studies of Northern Ghanian orature. And in art history, many Africanists have helped introduce ways of approaching artwork that take a rich and sophisticated account of cultural context.

Often it's when unfamiliar cultural formations are explored that the inadequacies of traditional disciplinary boundaries in the Western academy are most clearly revealed. The gap between the social sciences and the humanities is often bemoaned by those studying the complexities of African history and cultural forms. As Kwame Appiah observes in a recent grant proposal:

> Methods normally used in anthropology and in art history, for example, can provide profound and mutually reinforcing illumination of the cultural significance of a masquerade or the architecture of a shrine, but students and scholars who are taught to see these methods as radically incommensurable are bound to fail to achieve these insights.
>
> Those scholars who have faced up to these challenges have had to develop theoretical and methodological tools and data resources that promise help in thinking creatively about the ways in which society and culture relate to each other quite generally. In short, the challenges posed by (for example) African materials and the new approaches and techniques developed to deal with the varieties of African experience offer

an opportunity to enrich and expand the perspectives of all humanities disciplines and to aid in casting off disciplinary blinders.

In literary theory, our understanding of expressive acts and of the symbolic have been influenced by, for instance, Victor Turner's work on the Ndembu, and if you're reading a new historicist essay on drama in Renaissance England, don't be surprised to encounter references to Clifford Geertz's (1973) work on the Balinese. I don't want to exaggerate the gains; the opening up of traditional disciplines to the scholarly insights of the new has only just begun and hasn't progressed as far as it might have.

But I do want to emphasize that a true decentering of the humanities can't be just a matter of new content in old forms. We have to get away from the paradigm of disciplinary essentialism, imagining the boundaries of disciplines as hermetic, imagining our architectures of knowledge as natural or organic. Granted, sometimes conversation is neither possible nor productive. But we don't need a lazy sort of Platonism that can pretend to "cut nature at the joints"—sustaining the illusion only as long as we don't inquire too closely about the peculiar institutional history of our own particular discipline.

Solutions

I've suggested that moving toward this human notion of the humanities moves us away from the divisive us-and-them implications of traditional defenses of these studies and removes a source of cultural alienation that is clearly breeding disenchantment and disillusionment among those for whom the experience of higher education may matter the most. But I also think—and here my Whiggish triumphalism is revealed—that this notion is the natural conclusion of scholarly enlightenment in which ethnocentric presuppositions have fallen under scholarly critique (autocritique) and been found wanting. We need, for instance, to rethink the whole notion of comparative literature. The most influential and innovative programs in comparative literature have usually embraced just three languages: Latin, French, and German. I look forward to truly comparative programs that embrace the languages and literatures of Yoruba, Urdu, or Arabic as well as the traditional European languages and literatures. I think we should design a required humanities course that's truly humanistic—with the Western segment comprising a quarter or a third—in addition to the traditional Western civilization course, so that students can begin to understand the histories of civilization itself in a truly comparative manner. Such an embracive posture honors the best, the noblest traditions and ambitions of the academy, and while I've decried cultural nationalism, I hope you'll permit me to bow to it in citing something Ishmael Reed (1988) has said on the subject of multiculturalism. He said it's possible here "because the United States is unique in the world: The world is here" (p. 1).

Or listen to a great canonical author, Herman Melville ([1849] 1957), writing a century earlier:

> There is something in the contemplation of the mode in which America has been settled, that, in a noble breast, should forever extinguish the prejudices of national dislikes.
>
> Settled by the people of all nations, all nations may claim her for their own. You can not spill a drop of American blood without spilling the blood of the whole world. . . . We are not a narrow tribe of men, . . . No: our blood is as the flood of the Amazon, made up of a thousand noble currents, all pouring into one. We are not a nation, so much as a world [p. 162].

Now, it turns out that the affirmative action programs for recruiting minority faculty have only been successful at institutions where strong ethnic studies programs exist. Many ambitious "minority" scholars of my generation, feeling secure in their academic credentials and their ethnic identities, have tried to fill a lacuna they perceived in their own education by producing scholarship about, well, "their own people." A lot of the social commitment that emerged during the 1960s has been redirected toward the scholarly arena; continents of ignorance have been explored and charted. At the same time, minority studies (so called) are not "for" minorities, any more than "majority studies" (let's say) are for majorities. And it is wrong simply to confuse affirmative action objectives in employment with the teaching of such subjects.

I respect what Robert Nisbet (1973) calls the Academic Dogma—knowledge for its own sake (I suspect it doesn't quite exist, but that's another matter). At the same time, I believe that truly humane learning can't help but expand the constricted boundaries of human sympathy, of social tolerance. Maybe the truest thing to be said about racism is that it represents a profound failure of imagination. I've talked a good deal about multiculturalism as a good in itself, as the natural shape of scholarship untrammeled by narrow ethnocentrism, and also as a response to the persistence of racism on campuses. And the best ethnic studies departments have made a real contribution to this ideal of scholarly diversity. As I said, I respect the ideal of the disinterested pursuit of knowledge, however unattainable, and I don't think classes should be converted into consciousness-raising sessions, Lord knows; at the same time, anyone who's not a positivist realizes that "moral education" is a pleonasm. In the humanities facts and values don't exist in neatly disjunct regimes of knowledge. Allan Bloom (1987) is right to ask about the effect of higher education on our kids' moral development—even though that's probably the only thing he is right about.

Amy Gutmann (1980) said something important in her recent book *Democratic Education:* "In a democracy, political disagreement is not something that we should generally seek to avoid. Political controversies over our educational problems are a particularly important source of social progress because they have the potential for educating so many citizens" (p. 20). I think that's true. I think a lot of us feel that any clamor or conflict over the curriculum is just a bad thing in itself, that it somehow undermines the legitimacy of the institutions of knowledge. This constitutes a sort of no-news-is-good-news attitude on the subject of education; believers in it think that if you so much as look at a university cross-eyed, it'll dry up and blow away and then where will you be?

Actually, however, one of the most renewing activities we can do is to rethink the institutions where we teach people to think. We invest in myths of continuity, but universities have constantly been molting and creating themselves anew for the last millennium, and there's no reason to think that'll change in the next. Gerald Graff (1988) has been saying, where there's no consensus—and there *is* no consensus—teach the conflicts. In fact, I think at the better colleges we do. We don't seem to be able not to, and that's nothing to be embarrassed about; college isn't kindergarten, our job isn't to present a seemly, dignified, unified front to the students. College students are too old to form—we shouldn't delude ourselves—but they're not too old to challenge. I'm reminded of something that the college president and educator Robert Maynard Hutchins (1957) wrote in a book he published during the height of the McCarthy era. He recounted a conversation he'd had with a distinguished doctor about the attempt of the board of regents of the University of California to extort (as Hutchins put it) "an illegal and unconstitutional oath of loyalty from the faculty of that great institution." "Yes, but," the doctor said, "if we are going to hire these people to look after our children we are entitled to know what their opinions are." And Hutchins grandly remarks: "I think it is clear that the collapse of liberal education in the United States is related as cause or effect or both to the notion that professors are people who are hired to look after children" (p. 20). Wise words, those.

The Importance of Pluralism

In all events, the sort of pluralism I've been recommending has one evolutionary advantage over its opponents. If you ask how we form a consensus around such a "decentering" proposal, the answer is that it doesn't exactly require a consensus. Which is why, in the words of John Dewey ([1916] 1944), "pluralism is the greatest philosophical idea of our times." Not that this puts us home free. As Dewey also said:

What philosophers have got to do is to work out a fresh analysis of the relations between the one and the many. Our shrinking world presents that issue today in a thousand different forms. . . . How are we going to make the most of the new values we set on variety, difference, and individuality—how are we going to realize their possibilities in every field, and at the same time not sacrifice that plurality to the cooperation we need so much? How can we bring things together as we must without losing sight of plurality?

Learning without center is not learning without focus. We've all seen undigested eclecticism posing as a bold new synthesis, but to read and write culture anew means additional demands for rigor and coherence, not emancipation from these things. I take Dewey's question seriously, but there's nothing vaporous about the form the answer takes: It is made of brick and mortar and sometimes a little ivy about the architrave. For us—scholars and teachers—the answer is the university, whose constant refashioning is our charge, burden, and privilege.

References

Baldwin, J. *Notes of a Native Son.* Boston: Beacon Press, 1955.
"Blacks and Whites on the Campuses: Behind Ugly Racist Incidents, Student Isolation, and Insensitivity." *Chronicle of Higher Education,* April 26, 1990, p. A1.
Bloom, A. *The Closing of the American Mind.* New York: Simon & Schuster, 1987.
Dewey, J. *Democracy and Education: Introduction to the Philosophy of Education.* New York: Free Press, 1944. (Originally published 1916.)
Du Bois, W.E.B. *The Souls of Black Folk.* New York: Avon, 1965.
Eble, K. E. *Professors as Teachers.* San Francisco: Jossey-Bass, 1972.
Foucault, M. *Language, Counter-Memory, Practice.* (D. Bouchard and S. Simon, trans.) Ithaca, N.Y.: Cornell University Press, 1977.
Geertz, C. *The Interpretation of Cultures.* New York: Basic Books, 1973.
Graff, G. "What Shall We Be Teaching When There's No We." *Yale Journal of Criticism,* 1988, *1* (2), 189–211.
Gramsci, A. *Selections from the Prison Notebooks.* (Q. Hoare and G. N. Smith, eds.) New York: International Publishers, 1971.
Gutmann, A. *Democratic Education.* New York: Cambridge University Press, 1980.
Heidegger, M. *What Is Philosophy?* (W. Kluback and J. T. Wilde, trans.) Boston: Twayne, 1958.
Hutchins, R. M. *The Conflict in Education in Democratic Society.* New York: Harper & Row, 1957.
McFarland, T. *Shapes of Culture.* Iowa City: University of Iowa Press, 1987.
Marquand, R. "Racism on Campus: Part II." *Christian Science Monitor,* June 15, 1988, p. 3.
Melville, H. *Redburn: His First Voyage.* New York: Doubleday, 1957. (Originally published 1849.)
Nisbet, R. *The Degradation of the Academic Dogma.* New York: Basic Books, 1973.
Parry, M. *Comparative Research in Oral Traditions.* Columbus, Ohio: Slavica, 1987.

Press, R. M. "College Enrollment Rate for Black Students Is Falling." *Christian Science Monitor,* May 24, 1986, p. 4.

Reed, I. *Writin' Is Fightin'.* New York: Atheneum, 1988.

Wright, R. "White Man Listen." *Présence Africaine,* 1956, 2, 340–349.

Henry Louis Gates, Jr., is John Spencer Basset Professor of English at Duke University and was the W.E.B. Du Bois Professor of English at Cornell University until 1990.

Introducing cultural diversity into core curriculum courses need not be political.

Miss Grimp Revisited: Reconfiguring Composition, Literature, and Cultural Literacy

Feroza Jussawalla

> My broader philosophic bias is that I am a pluralist: I cannot conceive of any one way of teaching that will excel all others. Nor am I inclined toward insisting on those few things that must be taught as opposed to all those things that humans want to learn. Moreover, I see formal education as a means of respecting, drawing upon, passing along human diversity. But as firm as I am about this preference, I do not deny the appeal of the unifying idea as a way of ordering a world of diverse particulars. However, the importance of diversity over unity is what makes teaching different from writing or research.
> —Eble, 1988.

With graying braids wrapped around her head, the fin-de-siècle Miss Grimp flourished Wren and Martin's *English Grammer,* taught her students the names of various rivers from the Irawaddy to the Liffey, and held out the Salisbury Cathedral as the epitome of fine architecture. V. S. Naipaul (1987) documents how his English reader created in him a love of all things Western, with the Salisbury Cathedral not the least among them and Plato and Aquinas at the head of the list. In the continuing debate between the proponents of Western culture courses and the proponents of third world or cultural studies, the participants often forget how a love of culture is developed and how such a love is transmitted. In its politicized form, this debate leaves departments polarized and ignores the uses to which various texts, whether third world or not, can be put in curricula that must meet the challenges of today's world—a world in which an ayatollah puts a price on the head of a writer he disapproves of.

Literacy and Cultural Literacy

Despite the influential report by the National Commission on Excellence in Education (1983), "A Nation at Risk," increasing numbers of freshmen enter our universities reading at the ninth- or tenth-grade level and seem to come from varying interlingual or intercultural backgrounds. Along with examples of the lack of basic reading and writing skills, even Hirsch (1987) has documented examples of the inability of our students to pinpoint their hometowns on a map or to be aware of any information outside their own immediate environment. Not more than a few years ago, it was fashionable to conduct cultural literacy tests in the composition classroom with questions such as "Who was Michelangelo?" and "What religion was Jesus born into?" and to be appalled when students indicated that Jesus was born a Christian. While such examples underscore the need for students to learn about their own cultures, it seems even more compelling that in an increasingly complex world students understand the role of language and culture in global processes, at the same time that they become skilled in dealing with their own environments. Thus, a return to the Miss Grimp approach—teaching reading, writing, and culture in a general introductory way—would help us do what innumerable Miss Grimps did throughout the British empire: develop our students' awareness of their own cultures and contexts while at the same time developing a love of what Macaulay (cited in Parameswaran, 1976) imperiously called "our arts, our morals, our literature, and our laws." As a result of the spread of English, these aspects of "our" culture are now the shared consciousness of over half the world. In this chapter, I suggest that reconfiguring our traditional departmental structures to incorporate some third world studies at introductory levels and within the scope of traditional courses can lead back, interestingly or ironically, to the Macaulayan imperative.

Varieties of English and Bilingual Writers

As a lecturer teaching composition and a graduate student working on questions of English language use by third world writers, I found that many of the problems my students were having in their writing were questions that major writers from the third world had struggled with. How should they use and change English to express their own particular consciousness, whether they were an Anglo from West Texas or a Hispanic student writing in a second language? How could they make the transition into writing what was considered standard English? Or even start writing in what was acceptable English for their college teachers? In these teaching situations, literature written by contemporary Indian authors such as R. K. Narayan ([1935] 1980) or Raja Rao ([1938] 1963) or by contemporary West African writers such as Chinua Achebe ([1958] 1982) suddenly began to prove useful in the rather unlikely place of an English composition classroom in America. These writers had struggled with the same questions of how to use English in differing contextual situations. In their fiction, they gave voice to the varying uses of English from different parts of the world. These examples helped composition students in a beginning writing class make the transition from the personal voice to the public voice, a transition that composition theorists over the last decade have emphasized (Maimon and others, 1981). In thus teaching the importance of audience, composition teachers attempt to move students from expressive writing to transactional writing (Bridges and Lunsford, 1984). The first emphasizes the writer's personal expressive style and is often characterized by an English not considered standard, while the other reaches out to a wider audience and uses a style more widely accepted. The writing across the curriculum movement (Maimon and others, 1981) also attempted to address this issue of an appropriate English style, pointing out the difference between a scientific style that would be intelligible only to a small group and a style that could be accepted across all disciplines. Third world writers, in representing English as used in India or Nigeria versus a more international version of English, are essentially making the same choices about appropriateness. When I ask students to tell a story about their region that reflects the way English is used in, for example, the Southwest and then ask them to make it intelligible to the wider audience of their classmates, they come to see how their writing experience parallels that of others in other parts of the world. While this makes them conscious of English as the bridge to various cultures, it also emphasizes a commonality of experience that is helpful to our students. This is one basic way of putting third world literature to use in our already existing curriculum.

How Fiction Can Help

An example from the fiction of Indian writer R. K. Narayan ([1935] 1980) shows the difference between the "Indianized" English of Narayan's dialogue and the standard English of his narrative. While making a case for the appropriate use of English based on audience and situation, Narayan's work also provides an introduction to his culture, as the following narrative paragraph illustrates:

> Father was apparently deaf to Swaminathan's remarks. He stood over Swaminathan and set him to dust his books and clean his table. Swaminathan vigorously started blowing off the dust from the book covers.

He caught the spider carefully, and took it to the window to throw it out. He held it outside the window and watched it for a while. It was swinging from a strand that gleamed in a hundred delicate tints [p. 84].

Immediately after this, Narayan gives us the nativized form of English in India: "'Look sharp! Do you want a whole day to throw out the spider?' Father asked" (p. 84). And when Swami goes to his grandmother, they both use localized or nativized constructions (in italics here) in their speech. For example, rather than saying "Where can I find a piece of cloth?," Swami and his grandmother use the infinitive of the verb *go*:

"Granny, get me a piece of cloth, quick!"
"Where am I *to go for a piece of cloth*?"
"Where *am I to go*?" he asked peevishly.
He almost wept as he said: "I don't know what Rajam and Mani will think, *waiting for me there, if I keep on fooling here*. [This is a continuous participial construction typical of Indian English.] Granny, if Father cannot find any work to do, why shouldn't he *go and sleep*?" [Rather than "go to sleep"] [p. 85].

American students can take away from such an example both a sense of "their right to their own language" and the contexts in which this language is appropriate. For Swaminathan in this situation—an anglicized, Christian mission school student conversing with his grandmother who at best speaks some broken English—his own idiom is appropriate. For Narayan in the narrative, it is not. Therefore, as Weir (1982) has pointed out, "dialogue is of primary importance" (p. 310) in portraying the spoken language of the characters and their contexts. She is careful to point out that Narayan only varies his style when it is understood that the character is speaking in English or a form of it and not when the author is translating the character's speech. The example from Narayan is a perfect illustration of the difference between the personal voice and the public voice, between the colloquial dialogue and the more polished written narrative. It can also be used to illustrate the difference between students' personal writing and the formal writing necessary in academic situations.

Narayan's English sounds different from the English most of our students are used to. When they realize that English takes on the tint of the many countries in which it is spoken—that it becomes "nativized," as linguists have called it—and that this is legitimate in certain situations, they begin to see how this applies to their own use of English and to understand the way in which localisms or second-language structures influence the use of the language. Students learn to distinguish the way in which they use English, their particular local colloquialisms, from the way in which English is used in their textbooks or by their professors in specific disciplines. In addition, these insights help students get over their writing blocks, especially those connected with putting down their thoughts in formal or standard English.

Choosing an Appropriate Style

Thus, through the evaluation of such literary works, students become aware of the effect of the personal voice versus that of the transactional voice. They begin to see that a work like Tutuola's (1953) *The Palm-Wine Drinkard* uses the personal voice throughout, while a work like Narayan's *Swami and Friends* alternates between the transactional voice in the narrative and the personal, expressive voice in the characters' dialogue. This raises for students the issue of the communicability of the personal, expressive voice and is an important step for them in encouraging transactional writing. It makes them aware of the need for modulating the writer's voice based on audience, acceptability, and appropriateness. They see that Tutuola's *The Palm-Wine Drinkard* appeals to a limited audience because of its use of a purely personal voice, while Narayan's transactional narration, used in an attempt to communicate information, is addressed to a wider audience.

These examples show how literature written in English by writers from around the world helps the average American student find himself or herself in a community of writers all struggling to find their voice in English. As they see the different ways in which these authors have used the English language, students begin to be able to choose the appropriate style and tone for varying situations. This is a particularly nonthreatening way to introduce beginning writers to questions of audience and style. They even begin to understand the political phenomena of the spread of English and of the results of languages in contact. In addition, they are learning about different cultures and being exposed to new historical, geographical, and political facts—and thus developing a form of cultural literacy.

Cultural Literacy in Context

In a cross-registered writing-across-the-curriculum and political science class at the University of Texas at El Paso, the political science faculty member would routinely test students about current affairs and politics as depicted in the media. While students could often not name the home state of the vice-president of the United States, they were often able to name the candidates of the PRI and PAN parties of Mexico. This example shows the need to take the shared knowledge of varying contexts into consideration when determining what should constitute cultural literacy.

Thus, the introduction of literature by non-Western authors into the English composition classroom fulfills two related goals: those of cognitive development and of cultural literacy. The use of cross-cultural literature challenges the student who says, "I am monocultural and want my world to remain so," as it challenges the student who says, "I don't care about the way English is spoken in India, Nigeria, or anywhere else." It forces students to learn that there are different norms for different contexts, thus making them aware of speech and language communities across both cultures and disciplines.

Rhetoric, Culture, and Politics

Because of the colonial and postcolonial origins of much world literature in English and because of the multicultural nature of this literature and its authors, several of these works incorporate what one could call "the rhetoric of argument." The Ugandan writer Okot p'Bitek's *Song of Lawino and Song of Ocol* (1984) works perfectly in a class where students are writing an argument paper about women's issues. In this work, a rather Westernized African male expresses disenchantment with his wife for remaining traditionally African and "backward," as he sees it. A lively debate ensues about feminism and women's rights and about whether to adapt to Western ways or not.

Chinua Achebe's (1967) *A Man of the People* is a good example of the use of political rhetoric. Chief Nanaga, an adept politician, is skilled at persuading his constituents to vote for him despite his corrupt and nepotistic practices. One of the rhetorical skills he uses is language appropriate to the situation: He uses pidgin when talking to an urban audience, he switches back and forth between English and African languages when talking to his rural audiences, and he uses American English when commiserating with the Americans. This way of establishing himself as a "man of the people" is an important part of his persuasive tactics.

This material helps students recognize not just the techniques of effective persuasion and argumentation but also the techniques used by third world and other political leaders as they deal with contemporary American state departments. Thus, in addition to heightening students' knowledge and awareness of other cultures, it heightens their awareness of political processes. Perhaps a more culturally aware electorate could prevent such political and cross-cultural faux pas as sending McFarlane to Iran with a cake and a Bible.

Coming Home to the West

What is possibly most interesting about such an educational process is how it can lead back to an awareness of what we have come to call "Western cultural heritage." In "A Cultural Critic Answers His Own," Bloom (1989) tells us that an incident like the censuring of Rushdie by the ayatollah should take us back to reading Milton and Locke. On the other hand, I believe it may have been possibly Rushdie's overly Western education—public school at Rugby, a graduate education at Cambridge—and his belief in Western values that led him to offend the ayatollah without meaning to do so. Rushdie has frequently compared himself to Joyce, calling his writing style "post-Joycean" or "sub-Joycean," but if he had had adequate knowledge of his Indian and Islamic context, would he not have known that the Joycean option was not open to him? In contrast, where third world writers have shown awareness of both Western and non-Western traditions, they seem to have achieved a better balance in their writing and their worldview.

In teaching students about Narayan and answering why he writes in English, I point out Narayan's reading and education. In *My Days*, Narayan (1974) speaks of the writers who meant the most to him. He writes, "Tagore's poetry . . . swept me off my feet in those days. . . . So did much of Palgrave, Keats, Shelley, Byron, and Browning. They spoke of an experience that was real and immediate in my surroundings, and stirred in me a deep response" (p. 58). We find Naipaul (1987) expressing the same knowledge of and love for Western culture while showing an awareness of the oppression of the third world evidenced by colonial imperialism, the Dutch slave trade with Venezuela, and the settling of Trinidad by indentured labor brought from India. Naipaul was raised in the small colonial world of Trinidad and in a tiny Asian-Indian community, but he was also aware of the India of his grandfather as well as of the Orinoco of Columbus and Sir Walter Raleigh. By bringing this knowledge together with the Western intellectual tradition of his education, Naipaul in *An Enigma of Arrival* achieves a sort of homeostasis. But for Naipaul, Western culture is supreme.

On the basis of such examples, we can perhaps make another case for exposing our students to world traditions. If the juxtaposition of third world traditions and Western education led third world writers to develop a love of Western culture, then perhaps third world traditions will lead American students to hunger for knowledge about Western traditions and subsequently for knowledge of themselves. While this seems a rather circuitous route, perhaps it is the route to the new "Renaissance person."

Conclusion

In developing a global perspective for our students, we let them see the commonalities of all people's experience. In a technical world tied together not only by communications systems but also by the English language, underscoring these commonalities is much more important than setting up an opposition between the Western and the non-Western, the ideological and the nonideological. Thus, we need to reconfigure the ways in which we have taught traditional courses not only in order to expand the canon or to reinforce Western culture but in order to present our students with the tools they need to make sense of our complex world.

For all of these reasons, interweaving non-Western studies with existing core curricula is surely preferable to putting them in courses by themselves. The latter approach only becomes a way of marginalizing and ghettoizing third world studies, as well as the persons presumed qualified to teach them. Western consumers of third world culture need to be convinced that the third world speaks to them of a common experience, not of something "out there" that happens in countries riddled with coups and plagued by Marxist ideologies and dictatorial ayatollahs. Many departments have attempted to update their curricula superficially by looking specifically for a "person of color" (literally) to teach an added-on component to their "great civilizations" course. In this, Bloom (1989) is right in saying that universities have passed on their affirmative action complaints to the humanities. Instead of hiring a person of color to teach eighteenth-century studies, administrators presume that minorities are fit only to teach anglophone literature of the third world or world literature by people of color. Should their color be slightly lighter, we presume that they do not subscribe to the right shade of Marxist ideology. Third world studies have become too much the purview of the "exotic primitive," and their instrumental use in the already existing curricula is too often ignored. What we need, then, is to reconfigure the traditional disciplinary breakdowns in order to bring third world studies into the mainstream of higher education.

References

Achebe, C. *A Man of the People*. New York: Anchor, 1967.
Achebe, C. *Things Fall Apart*. London: Heinemann, 1982. (Originally published 1958.)
Bloom, A. "A Cultural Critic Answers His Own." *Wall Street Journal*, March 30, 1989, p. A12.
Bridges, C. W., and Lunsford, R. *Writing: Discovering Form and Meaning*. Belmont, Calif.: Wadsworth, 1984.
Eble, K. E. *The Craft of Teaching: A Guide to Mastering the Professor's Art*. (2nd ed.) San Francisco: Jossey-Bass, 1988.
Hirsch, E. D., Jr. *Cultural Literacy: What Every American Needs to Know*. Boston: Houghton Mifflin, 1987.
Maimon, E., Belcher, G., Hearn, G., Nobine, B., and O'Connor, F. W. *Writing in the Arts and Sciences*. Boston: Little, Brown, 1981.
Naipaul, V. S. *The Enigma of Arrival*. New York: Knopf, 1987.
Narayan, R. K. *My Days*. New York: Viking Penguin, 1974.
Narayan, R. K. *Swami and Friends*. Chicago: University of Chicago Press, 1980. (Originally published 1935.)
Parameswaran, U. *A Study of Representative Indo-English Novelists*. New Delhi, India: Vikas, 1976.
p'Bitek, O. *Song of Lawino and Song of Ocol*. Portsmouth, N.H.: Heinemann Educational Books, 1984.
Rao, R. *Kanthapura*. New York: New Directions, 1963. (Originally published 1938.)
Tutuola, A. *The Palm-Wine Drinkard*. New York: Grove, 1953.
Weir, A. L. "Style Range in New English Literatures." In B. Kachru (ed.), *The Other Tongue*. Urbana: University of Illinois Press, 1982.

Feroza Jussawalla is associate professor of English and director of the honors program at the University of Texas at El Paso.

The coaching model applied to a first-year community college writing class elucidates the role of the coach, the players, the team, the process, and finally the "big games"—formal graded research papers.

A Coaching Model for the Teaching of Writing

Anthony J. Walsh

> My curiosity about teaching has caused me to poke around outside my own discipline of English into fields besides the humanities and beyond my own experience.
> —Eble, 1988.

While there are some obvious differences between how a team is selected and how a student population is selected, the coaching model offers valuable insight into how skills are learned, polished, and finally mastered under pressure. This insight provides considerable guidance for the teaching and learning process in general and for the teaching of writing in particular. This chapter describes the application of the coaching model to a first-year community college writing class.

The model revolves around the following key elements: (1) practice and drill (nongraded exercises); (2) fouling out (performance evaluation); (3) playbook and plays (information resources and writing strategies); (4) big games (formal graded research papers); and (5) the postmortem (review of research papers and more practice and drill).

It is important to clarify the various relationships in this model before going any further. The professor is obviously the coach; his or her role is to set limits and goals, determine the various strategies, schedule the "big games," and evaluate performance for both the team as a whole and for individual players. The player's role is to attend all sessions, master the various skills and plays, cooperate with other team members while at the same time competing with them for individual recognition, and be prepared to accept criticism without becoming discouraged. The coach's objective is to develop the team to the point where it can make decisions and solve writing problems spontaneously with only a minimum of guidance.

It is obvious that the members of a classroom team are much more heterogeneous in terms of skill levels than the members of an athletic team usually are. Still, in both cases, all team members have some basic skills to build on; in the classroom, for example, they all speak English, and they all can write, even if only at an elementary level. Like the athletic coach, the writing coach must not only develop new skills in the team members but also overcome their years of practicing bad habits. Can the writing levels of the team be raised without going back over formal grammar, something they have been exposed to for much of the previous twelve years and apparently never mastered? This approach assumes that the answer is "yes." If speech can be learned without a knowledge of formal rules, then it should be possible to improve written expression simply through practice and drill, careful coaching, and constant monitoring. For example, it is not necessary to know why "ain't ain't right" to eliminate the practice; it is only necessary to make its use costly to the user in order to bring about the desired change. Thus, just as repeated misjudgments in an athletic contest can get a player thrown out of a game, so repeated misjudgments in writing will earn the ultimate disapproval, a failing grade. It is the coach's job to prepare the players so that F's are the exception rather than the rule.

Practice and Drill

Under the coaching model, practice and drill sessions are always spontaneous—that is, there is never advance notice of the topic to be addressed. These sessions are usually initiated by watching a ten-minute film. The students are asked to write a short summary of the film and describe its main thesis. Few instructions are given, as the objective is to observe the skill levels and natural tendencies of the players under unstructured conditions. The use of films tests simultaneously for a variety of skills, such as listening, note taking, perception, and general attention and focusing ability.

Just as the coach of an athletic team not only expects the players to perform during the practice and drill sessions but also knows that he or she will have to demonstrate correct technique, so, too, the writing coach will need to give demonstrations. The coach might give a clinic for the team's benefit, for example, by asking the players to suggest a research topic that the coach will then sketch out on the spot. During this clinic, the coach can demonstrate several aspects of the writing process, such as how to define and refine a topic, how to outline the task, how to brainstorm, how to use the library to research the topic, how to create a topic sentence, and, of course, how to write a coherent paragraph. If such a clinic is given at the beginning of the term, it can provide a helpful model for the team throughout the course.

The practice and drill sessions are the most important element in the coaching model. The short-duration exercises get everyone writing. None of these exercises is formally graded, but all are reviewed while they are being written. The coach, walking up and down the aisles to observe the players' writing, uses these sessions to make a quick assessment of the progress of the team and to note specific, common writing problems. He or she selects examples of either good writing or "good" errors—that is, errors with high instructional value—and asks these students to present their work during the team review. The coach also gives the players instant feedback on their level of performance, advises them of problems, and presents them with a variety of possible solutions. Then, without warning, the coach stops the exercise and begins a review.

The review has two parts: The coach addresses common problems and makes suggestions for improvements in these areas, and then the volunteers present their work to the team for analysis or resolution. The team is expected to make suggestions for solving the specific problems. Each suggestion is tested within the context of the original sentence or paragraph to see if it improves the level of expression or alters it. As the term goes on and everyone becomes comfortable with the process, team members should begin to volunteer their work without prompting by the coach. At this point, the coach functions more as a consultant who guides the discussion lest a new error be learned and incorporated into someone's repertoire.

Based on these practice and drill exercises, the team develops a list of "fatal flaws," which function much as fouls do in basketball; if these flaws appear under game conditions, they will result in the ultimate disapproval. Team members are required to keep a list of these fatal flaws, which grows as the term progresses. They are constantly reminded of the importance of avoiding any of these errors in their formal work. At first, many may think that their errors will not be noticed or that the penalty will not be as severe as has been stated. But after the first formal paper has been graded, all these mistaken beliefs are usually abandoned, and the players become sensitive to their manner of expression, even though they may not understand *why* a certain flaw is "fatal."

Each practice session builds on the previous ones, both reviewing familiar tasks and introducing new ones to be mastered. The coach must constantly remind the team that the errors made in these sessions will not be tolerated in formal situations and that the practice and drill are merely rehearsals for the big games. Just as in athletics, there are far more practice sessions than there are games.

Fouling Out

Throughout the practice and drill sessions, the coach continuously evaluates each player's writing so that each player becomes aware of problems as they arise. The players are required to keep, in addition to the list of fatal flaws, lists of both the general team problems and of their personal ones. Before any formally graded assignment is given, these lists are reviewed and the fatal flaws list is written on the board. The team is given an opportunity to seek help with any item on any list. Players are reminded of the consequences of poor performance, which helps motivate them to become active participants in the review.

The first "games" are minor assignments with the topic provided by the coach; freelance playing is not allowed. Players on an athletic team do not choose their own plays but must innovate under game pressure within a carefully prescribed set of guidelines; in much the same way, the writing coach guides the actions of his or her players. Since all writing is done in the classroom, the coach can provide guidance during the process without interfering with the validity of the exercise. For example, the writing coach may point out to a player that he or she has an agreement problem, a voice problem, or a spelling problem in the assignment. The player must find the problem and take immediate corrective action lest it lead to a foul. A single minor infraction will not cause a player to foul out, but an accumulation of them will. Of course, a fatal flaw will earn immediate dismissal from the game—an F.

Once this first assignment has been completed, graded, and returned, the coach initiates a game review. This review focuses first on common errors and then on individual errors, and these errors provide the basis for the next practice and drill sessions.

Retraining

Armed with new insights into the writing process and its pitfalls, the team is ready to resume its training. Timeouts are now introduced into the sessions as a way of enhancing the teaching and learning process. The team is once again given short practice and drill exercises, and the coach once again roams the aisles while carefully scrutinizing the work. Whenever an undesirable pattern is detected, a time-out is declared and everyone stops writing. The particular sentence or passage is then either read aloud or written on the board, and the team is asked to identify the problem. The identification need not be expressed in technical terms as long as the error is correctly detected, since the objective is to create an awareness of poor writing with or without any understanding of the formal rules involved. Once the error has been identified, the coach encourages the team to suggest alternative ways to resolve the difficulty. The author evaluates these suggestions in terms of the intent of the original statement. If the suggestions change the intent, then they are rejected; if they are consistent with the original intent, they are further evaluated in terms of what the author feels best or most clearly conveys the intended meaning. The coach obviously has a major role to play in this process.

One technique that has proved quite valuable in helping the players assess the impact of any given change on the overall meaning of the author's original statement is flowcharting. Sentences can be set up with the key elements presented as decision points, and each suggestion for a change can be considered a decision that has implications for everything that has gone before or will come after that point. For example, if there is a problem with inconsistency of voice within a paragraph, any one of the verbs could be changed, but that requires that all the others be changed to agree with it. The team and the "offending" player must decide which element to change, and the flowchart helps them to visualize the final outcome much as an athletic coach's X's and O's help team members visualize plays.

If errors are made during this stage of the process, they have no consequences, though the coach points them out and corrects them. Again the team is reminded that such tolerance exists only during practice sessions and that those same errors under game conditions could result in fouling out.

One other innovation introduced during this stage of the process is the ability to substitute players. During these practice and drill sessions, papers are often exchanged before they are completed, and another player is required to complete the essay without any loss of meaning, much as players are required to substitute for one another on an athletic team. This often creates much anguish for both players, since neither has had an opportunity to finish her or his own assignment and must now complete an essay that is foreign in terms of style and content. But this exercise requires players to develop much more versatility than would be the case if they only worked on their own products. They develop an insight into the thought processes of other writers, an appreciation of other ways of presenting the same idea, and a heightened awareness of the flow of language, since they must maintain that flow as they complete the assignment.

After several cycles of these practice sessions and minor graded assignments, the team must begin its preparation for the big game.

Playbook and Plays

In some respects, a whole sports season exists only for the end-of-season tournament—the big game. This is equally true for the writing class. Its whole season is oriented toward the final formal research paper. The preparation for this culminating event includes mastering the information resources (playbook) and the writing strategies (plays).

The team is introduced to the main information resource—the library—under highly controlled conditions. Each assignment is narrowly focused and requires intensive use of only one resource element. For example, the coach might assign a topic that requires the use only of microfilm resources, of biographical resources, or of the slide collection.

The library staff reinforce this approach by giving a series of short, highly focused orientations that complement the specific assignment. In this way, the library staff function much like assistant coaches who help to prepare the team for the big game. Throughout this process, the team is constantly coached through the playbook until the players are so familiar with the information resources or data base that using these resources has become second nature to them.

The team is given instruction in the fundamentals of the game, such as the reference and search systems, various styles of documentation, bibliography, and forms of note taking. As the players acquire mastery of the playbook and its contents, they are simultaneously practicing plays—various research and writing strategies. To ensure that these skills and strategies are mastered, the coach reminds the players that during the writing phase of the project—the game—they will not be allowed to use texts but must rely on their own handwritten notes or photocopies of pertinent pages. This rule encourages the players to be selective, just as athletes must select their shots carefully if they are to succeed under game conditions. If players bring texts with them to the big game, they are confiscated as illegal substances. Of course, unlike their counterparts in athletics, these texts must be returned when the game is over.

Big Games

As was the case in the practice and drill sessions, all writing on the end-of-term paper is done in the classroom under the coach's close supervision. This is to prevent the entrance of "ringers" into the game. This does not mean that players cannot practice on their own outside the scheduled times. In fact, they are encouraged to do just that with the clear understanding that they will start each formal session with a clean sheet of paper and may not simply copy what they allegedly did outside of class. The result of this tightly controlled writing environment is that players must demonstrate their own virtuosity under game conditions. Many players object to this system and often try to smuggle in finished products to be copied surreptitiously in class. These materials are confiscated, and the offending players are directed to reproduce the original as nearly as possible. The coach makes clear to them that the two papers will be compared, and they will be expected to explain any serious discrepancies. If there are too many discrepancies and the players are unable to explain them satisfactorily, they will be ejected from the game for being in possession of an illegal substance. Since all the rules of the game were clearly spelled out beforehand, players cannot protest the outcome.

Time-outs are once again employed during these game sessions, only now it is the players who call them. If players are experiencing difficulty with any phase of the game, they may signal to the coach that they wish a time-out in order to consult with the coach about the situation. The coach's role now is to guide the players through the problem by helping them see it more clearly and articulate alternative approaches, just as they did during the practice and drill sessions. The players must generate the alternatives, evaluate them, and select and apply what appears to be the best one. The coach may not indicate either approval or disapproval at this point; that comes later when the paper is formally evaluated and graded.

Postmortem

After graded papers are returned, the coach presents the team with an overall analysis of the most common errors and suggests a variety of strategies for addressing them. The examples that are used are taken directly from papers submitted but without attribution to any player. The team is then encouraged to evaluate the alternatives and to select the ones they believe would best correct the situation without altering the original intent of the writer. This approach helps to reinforce the lessons of earlier practice and drill sessions that the players are supposed to employ during the big games.

In addition to the common errors, the coach and the players also bring up specific errors during the postmortem. Players who are anxious to correct their misjudgments will volunteer their own errors, without hesitation or embarrassment, for team consideration. The team collaborates on the analysis and on acceptable solutions, while the coach guides the process and points out any unrecognized problems in the suggested solutions. In addition to asking for assistance in resolving errors, many players will ask for help in raising the level of their play, even though it is already technically correct.

At the conclusion of the postmortem, the team and the coach return to the practice and drill sessions in order to address specific problems and to raise the game to a higher level. This process continues until the term finally ends and the team disbands. Whatever the outcome, the coach always has the last word: "Wait till next season!"

Reference

Eble, K. E. *The Craft of Teaching: A Guide to Mastering the Professor's Art.* (2nd ed.) San Francisco: Jossey-Bass, 1988.

Anthony J. Walsh is on the faculty at Hudson Valley Community College in Troy, New York, and has received the Hudson Valley President's Award for Excellence in Teaching.

In its construction of the neutral and "free" classroom, dominant pedagogy produces positions from which the existing political and economic arrangements of late capital are viewed as natural and inevitable. Oppositional pedagogy resists this inevitability.

The Politics of the Classroom: Toward an Oppositional Pedagogy

Minette Marcroft

> A conscious attempt to be impersonal, dispassionate, and totally objective is likely to work more harm than good. . . . Arguing that a teacher can have opinions and convictions but denying them a place in the classroom robs both student and teacher of a valuable means of fostering learning.
> —Eble, 1988.

As the 1990s begin, it may seem that the conditions under which teachers and intellectuals labor are worse than ever. The university, as one of the targets of a neoconservative assault on the "excesses" of the liberal state, has been charged with abandoning its proper role. Allan Bloom, E. D. Hirsch, William Bennett, and other self-appointed guardians of hegemony have charged the academy with moral and intellectual "failures" spawned by "sixties radicalism" and the supposed anarchy of the current curriculum debate. These charges have become so routine that they have acquired respectability even in their most hysterical form; the *New York Times* (Rosenblatt, 1990) treats *Tenured Radicals* (Kimball, 1990)—a book that hallucinates an American academy controlled by feminist-Marxist-black-homosexual semioticians out to destroy "our free society"—as though it contained the horrible truth.

These accusations draw power from the conservative backlash of the late eighties, a backlash that included systemic legislative attacks on civil rights as well as increased acts of "random" violence against individual blacks, gays, and other minorities. When Jesse Helms and other bandwagoners protest the exhibition of works by Robert Mapplethorpe, Andres Serrano, Dread Scott, and David Wojnarowicz by limiting the funding of cultural production and when their student counterparts protest the existence of black and gay studies programs by slipping hate mail under doors, beating up black students, and decorating campuses with graffiti celebrating AIDS, they are all enforcing the same political agenda: The public spaces of "our free society" must be kept free from the intrusion of "special interests"—those who don't belong there. In other words, those cultural institutions through which the social and political legitimacy of dominant interests is ensured must at all costs be seen as neutral; the voices that challenge this neutrality must be silenced.

In the sphere of education, the "threat" to this neutrality has mostly been seen to come from the recent attempts to make changes in the traditional humanities curriculum. As the authoritative canon of great works is criticized for its ideological exclusiveness, the critics propose a multiculturalism as its replacement, arguing for greater inclusiveness as the antidote for historical exclusions. Both conservative and liberal positions are alike here in assuming that the political agenda of the university will be significantly altered by changes made in the content of education, that the addition of "famous new methods," in Althusser's (1971) words, will transform the ideological work of the school. These additions may effect various local reforms within disciplines, but a radical transformation of the institution involves changes at the level of the modes of production of knowledge and, ultimately, changes in the social relations and economic modes of production of which those discourses privileged as "knowledge" are an effect and reproduction. To begin an inquiry aimed at such transformations requires rethinking "knowledge" not just as a simple content that can be added to different institutional spaces without change but as inseparable from the form of its transmission, the material and discursive conditions of its production, reproduction, circulation, and consumption. It requires giving attention to how the site of learning, the classroom, is conventionally constructed and understood and recognizing the vital role these constructions play in the legitimation of the educational institution. After all, it is by permitting academic freedom in the classroom that the academy is commonly understood to be ethically tolerant and universally benevolent. But it is precisely in these dominant constructions of the classroom as an "unlimited" space of freedom, autonomy, and neutrality that the political and cultural limits of the academy are found, limits that strictly restrain the content of learning from potentially spilling over and intervening in existing social arrangements.

The Corporate University and the Production of Knowledge

Although in often limited and fragmented ways, the challenges to the hegemony of the traditional liberal arts curriculum have opened up a space for inquiry into the contemporary academy's social investment in both its ideological value and its connection to other political institutions and economic sites. In America, the late twentieth century has seen the decline of the traditional liberal arts academy funded through philanthropic endowments and governmental support and the rise of the corporate university—an institution increasingly supported by multinational conglomerates, the military-industrial complex, and international aid agencies and penetrated by their needs and interests in preserving a global economic and political status quo. Institutional changes in the corporate university, like the massive expansion of the applied sciences (and their population by students from third world economies) or the development of communication and media studies, are responses to the transition of capital to its late phase. This phase is marked by the shift of industrial production to third world sites, the expansion of capital into needed markets abroad, the development of a service-based domestic economy, and the explosion of electronic information and mass media technologies.

The resulting intensified instrumentalization of knowledge has transformed the agenda of higher education. Earlier promotion by liberals of the free and disinterested pursuit of knowledge has been superseded; the corporate university primarily funds and develops only those technical and theoretical knowledges specifically required by capitalism. As a result, what counts as "knowledge" is less defined by a concern with truth or liberal notions of the socially useful and more according to a pragmatic focus on managerial and organizational skills—skills needed to make adjustments within existing social arrangements for their smoother operation and efficiency.

This subordination of all knowledge to the requirements of existing conditions is shaped by what Ernest Mandel (1975) calls the ruling "technologism" of late capitalism: a belief in the ability of the existing social order to find a technical solution to all its contradictions. "The most obvious expression of this 'belief in organization' is the late capitalist ideal of a 'regimented society,' in which everyone has (and keeps) his place, while visible (and invisible) regulators ensure the steady and continuous growth of the economy. . . . The 'robustly individualistic industrial pioneer' is replaced by a 'team of experts' " (p. 500).

As the "robust industrial pioneer" gives way to the "team of experts," the notions of freedom in the corporate university shift as well. The autonomous humanist subject of the liberal arts academy, who freely pursues his or her self-determined goals and shapes his or her own destiny, gives way to a fragmented and administered subject, a problem solver focused on fixing disruptions in contemporary existence efficiently, not on "inefficiently" questioning the reason for such problems—a subject for whom freedom is increasingly only a component of private life where freedom equals the freedom of choice asserted through the pleasures of consumption.

The corporate university is one instance of the interpenetration of economic, political, and ideological spheres that characterizes late capitalist society. The growing contradictions between a more diverse and thorough domination by a multinational commodity economy and the continued claim to an unrestricted freedom by the Western democratic state are partly responsible for the postmodern crisis in the way humanist culture and its institutions are understood. In the face of this crisis, the need for the dominant discourses to rework and resecure institutional categories of neutrality and impartiality is greater than ever, and recent renovations in the existing repertoire of pedagogic constructions of the classroom are an effort to accomplish these goals.

Hegemonic Pedagogy and the Ethics of "Neutrality"

The ideological agenda of the academy is secured in many ways—in curriculum decisions, hiring practices, administrative policies, but most powerfully through its construction of the classroom. In educational theory and popular thought, the classroom holds a special place as an idealized site of learning, a place where students and teachers come together in the free pursuit of knowledge. The classroom is "where it all happens"; as a recent review of a book on teaching put it, "education . . comes down to one classroom, one teacher, and the small victories she and her students can claim as theirs alone" (Hancock, 1990, p. 75). It is this "aloneness" that characterizes the common understanding of the freedom of the classroom; separated from outside influences, individual students and teachers "own" the classroom's institutional connections and its connections to other social sites produces the classroom as an ahistorical, autonomous, and neutral space where the only limits on its freedom are the individual desires and abilities of the students themselves.

Though conventionally represented as on opposite ends of the spectrum, both traditional humanist pedagogy and newer variations influenced by post-industrial theory are alike in their construction of the classroom as such an apolitical and autonomous space. The strategies used to produce this neutrality may vary, but as Mas'ud Zavarzadeh (1989) argues, hegemonic pedagogies are united in their attempt "to remove all traces of their own historical constructedness and their limits as cultural and thus political institutions" (p. 51). In order to claim the authority of neutrality, hegemonic pedagogy "represents itself as the autonomous search for knowledge and attempts to erase all of its connections with the dominant economic practices which in fact determine what it 'discovers' as 'truth' and legitimates as 'knowledge'" (p. 53).

The Classroom of Traditional Pedagogy

In traditional pedagogy, the political neutrality of the classroom and therefore its morality are the results of its status as a "natural" site. Here teachers, those who naturally know more, distill skills and knowledge to students, who naturally know less. This asymmetry between the roles of student and teacher is grounded in a developmental psychology that explains this positioning as "natural": Students are emotionally and psychologically immature, underdeveloped young people who, almost organically, mature and grow with the help of older, more experienced role models. Learning thus has its seasons, and students cannot be forced too early into things they are not ripe for.

In this classroom, the teacher is called on to nurture students, performing the traditional role of midwife to knowledge: She or he helps students find or discover their own meanings. The knowledge born in this classroom is the free expression of the autonomous self's experience. The traditional understanding of a "good" teacher is therefore one who respects students' opinions and helps foster a democratic and pluralistic atmosphere by ensuring that in the classroom everyone's point of view gets included. Protecting and allowing individual experience, expressed through personal opinion, is both the guarantee and the limit of freedom in this classroom. To go beyond a simple pluralist inclusion, perhaps by raising questions about the relations between views included or by inquiring into the limits of inclusion, is impossible since the status of personal opinion is beyond question. Opinion is doubly protected from inquiry: As an innate given, individuals just *have* opinions—that is, its existence is transparent—and as the source of the individual's freedom ("nobody influences me, I make up my own mind"), it cannot morally be interfered with. Issues concerning the relationship between freedom and possession assumed by this notion of opinion and its relation to other notions of property and freedom, like the freedom derived from private property, are never raised. In this way, the classroom's own implication in the social arrangements that depend on these property relations is sealed off from scrutiny.

In its reliance on the "natural" division of power between young and old, the traditional classroom reproduces the relations of another dominant site of naturalized power relations—the family. So natural is this equation between classroom and family that liberal progressive educational theory often conceives of the most liberating classroom as one that has replaced a stern father figure with a benevolent mom (Walkerdine, 1986). Like the supposedly feminist arguments now embellishing management theory, which make a case for the inclusion of women in corporate hierarchy because they are innately more humane bosses, these assumptions fail to acknowledge the dominant uses of authority that define power as a natural attribute. Whether or not the teacher offers her or his help in a sympathetic way, the relation between student and teacher remains repressively paternal: Like a child, the student needs the moral protection and guidance of higher authorities who "naturally" act in his or her best interest.

The traditional classroom is a "familiarizing" classroom in the sense that it proposes that the concepts around which it is structured, like the humanist self, are natural or culturally neutral; it recirculates familiar notions of freedom, individuality, and responses to authority. In the traditional classroom, the teacher is granted and assumes authority, but the source of this authority is not examined. In other words, the power relations that construct authority—both the teacher's and that of others in society—are backgrounded, left unaccounted for, unexplained. As a result, the liberal teacher can pretend to suspend this authority, constructing himself or herself not as authority figure but as friend and making assertions that "we're all in this together," without examining how "we" might all be in this in quite different ways.

Within the traditional classroom, examining the classroom itself (as text, as cultural site, as pedagogical construction) is either seen as unnecessary or as not a part of the class's legitimate object of study. To make visible the different positions students occupy in relation to the dominant discourses in which the classroom exists—for example, to call attention to the forced bilinguality of urban black students—is, in the traditional understanding, to bring something into the classroom that isn't or shouldn't be there. And inquiring into the ideological production of categories like "individuality" or "opinion" is seen as a violent threat to students' natural individuality because such inquiry suggests that students are not freely in control of their destiny; it does not reassure students about who they are but in fact calls into question the status of "being someone."

Freedom and Choice in the Decentered Classroom

By drawing on postmodern theories of the subject and on poststructural critique of logocentric Western metaphysics, poststructuralist pedagogy aims to decenter traditional pedagogic paradigms, to show supposedly stable certainties, such as "self," "authority," and "meaning," to be in fact uncertain, indeterminate, and ever-changing. In this classroom the effects of decentering are valued for the change they bring, a change that does "not solve the old problems but exchanges them for an entirely new set of problems" (Ulmer, 1985, p. xiv). The decentered classroom addresses the crisis of the humanist subject in postmodern culture by problematizing subjectivity—that is, by raising questions about the subject's positioning in culture—but its pedagogic aim is not to solve but to suspend the closure that answers to these questions would provide.

Although valorizing change, such a pedagogy of questions is committed to a conservative political agenda because it amounts to the deferral of social change, of making up one's mind. This pedagogy can exist happily within the pluralist academy since it stops at the level of questioning and refuses to engage with answers. In many ways it is the liberal pluralist pedagogy par excellence, since with its eclectic assortment of contemporary theories, Saussurian linguistics, psychoanalysis, deconstruction, feminism, and so on, it claims to include all positions and exclude none. Of course, it does exclude. In excluding answers it draws strict boundaries around what sort of questions it permits. Those positions or questions that can be easily added to the existing configuration of knowledges without pressuring that configuration to change are accepted; those positions that pressure the entire configuration by insisting on the ends and effects of knowledge are not allowed.

Although the decentering classroom draws on an assortment of cultural theories to demystify and change the subject, it begs the question of "change for what?" Decentering the subject merely in order to offer students a way to exchange their opinions for new ones, to choose among an open-ended range of new subject positions, merely recirculates a pluralist endorsement of all positions as equally valuable and attainable. This decentering, by eliding the ways in which individual identity is substantially fixed, limited, and defined through the social and economic privilege some discourses have over others, produces an idealistic and ahistorical understanding of subjectivity, for not every position *is* equally available to all. In fact, it is only from the most culturally privileged set of positions that it may seem this way.

In decentering the subject within the self-liberating space of the autonomous classroom, this pedagogy reproduces the logic of the consumer marketplace with its smorgasbord of choices the consumer-student can freely partake of. Poststructuralist pedagogy is thus a pedagogy of consumerist pleasure, the pleasure of the new, of the different, of accumulation of the new and different. The pursuit of this kind of pleasure is never made uncomfortable by sustained inquiry into the politics of pleasure, since it is implicitly justified as ethical, as a mark of individual freedom, of the liberty of free choice. The decentered classroom is, in effect, an updated, high-tech version of the traditional classroom. Though it may raise issues of the subject in a different manner than humanist pedagogy does, it does not produce a qualitatively different subject, for its goal, too, is the transhistorical "free" subject who exercises his or her freedom through individual choice.

That this kind of pedagogy, although theoretical, rigorous, and unfamiliar, can become popular among teachers and students working within the most culturally and economically privileged institutions is not surprising, since it allows participants to feel cognitively sophisticated and up to date, reassuring them of their "superior" position as cultured and educated. And since it, like traditional pedagogy, constructs the autonomous classroom as a privileged site in which the pleasureful changes of the postmodern can be experienced, it reinforces existing divisions between public and private that prevent any pressure or inquiry that may arise in one space from contaminating other spaces. A postmodern male can enjoy the subversive pleasure of instability via *l'ecriture feminine* in class and then return to his apartment and enjoy the pleasures of stability afforded him by his wife and home.

In the hegemonic construction of the "free" classroom, then, regardless of local pedagogic variations, an unexamined eclecticism masks the ideological role the production of knowledge plays in the reproduction of social arrangements. By presenting the classroom as a politically neutral site where all points of view are tolerantly included, the contradictions between views are suppressed, and any notion of the social terrain as one of contested interests is avoided. Although critical theories or political pedagogical approaches may be incorporated into this classroom, their appropriation is conditioned by this pluralist eclecticism, which severs particular theories from the contexts of broader critical analysis (Glazer, 1987). A typical example of the recuperating effects of pluralist inclusion is the fate of Paolo Freire's pedagogical theory in many North American classrooms. Freire's (1970) theory of self-education and empowerment was originally developed in the context of the class struggle of an illiterate, rural South American peasantry against their aristocratic (and U.S.-backed) economic oppressors. This pedagogy of the oppressed has now become "the Freirian system" and has been imported to the "neutral" classroom of the U.S. university with no acknowledgment of the massive contradictions that exist between empowering a nonliterate people to struggle actively for control of the means of production and empowering a culturally privileged, mainly white North American middle-class student body to grab ever more entirely their "piece of the pie."

The Classroom as a Critique of Freedom

Whether pedagogical practices acknowledge it or not, then, they all make politically interested assumptions about meaning and reality; they propose a sense of the world and of our place in it. As an intervention into the production of meaning, which asks in whose interest, at the expense of whom, and for what uses meaning is produced, an oppositional pedagogy addresses the dominant constructions of "freedom" and "choice" in order to contest the vision of students as accepting subjects who "freely choose" existing social relations. The "defamiliarizing" classroom this pedagogy produces calls attention to itself as a cultural construction, and the actions within it are not spontaneous and free but are defined by and understood through their relations to social discourses. In this classroom, the teacher does not attempt to background or smooth over the conflicts and antagonisms between various positions or opinions in order to allow each position its place, but he or she attempts to explain such conflicts in relation to larger social antagonisms.

In order to make visible the ideological construction of meaning, oppositional pedagogy is concerned with inquiring into how students know what they know, why they seem to know some things in particular and not others, and what interests are served and supported by this unquestioned knowing. Therefore, rather than assuming the student already possesses her or his "own" knowledge and constructing the classroom along the lines of a free market, a site for the exchange and consumption of these fixed properties, oppositional pedagogy inquires into *whose* knowledge the students' "own" consists of and what the consequences of "owning" various knowledges are. This line of inquiry raises questions about the production and distribution of knowledge and makes possible other modes of production.

Rather than "respecting" opinion (that is, placing it beyond inquiry), oppositional pedagogy has a particular investment in a critique of opinion. Acknowledging both the ideological power of opinion and the student's potential for confronting this power, for recognizing and critiquing his or her own position, actually treats students with a much more enabling respect than a pedagogy that naturalizes their subordination.

In this defamiliarizing classroom, the teacher calls attention to herself or himself as teacher, impelling recognition of the institutionally and culturally prescribed authority of her or his role. Unlike the teacher in the familiarizing classroom, this teacher does not deny or "disown" her or his institutionally mandated authority or attempt to conceal the ways in which she or he is positioned differently from the students. The teacher instead makes visible the construction of his or her position through institutional practices and argues for his or her particular authority according to how he or she makes use of it; in other words, the teacher addresses directly the issue of the ends for which authority is used. By making authority and the power relations that construct the classroom visible, the teacher allows authoritative discourses to be contested. The classroom in which the teacher disowns authority—by pretending that he or she has none, is positioned just like the students, and equally shares their knowledge—is in fact authoritarian, since it functions to keep the discourses of authority hidden and unquestioned.

This kind of critique of the uses of authority is itself often glibly labeled authoritarian, and the teacher who works to introduce her or his students to counterhegemonic positions from which to critique the naturalization of exploitation and repression is often accused of "crushing" students with hard ideas or of willfully making things "too difficult." These tendencies to label and accuse indicate the academy's anxiety over having its own agenda questioned. By arguing for her or his particular use of authority, the oppositional teacher further violates the "neutrality" of the institution by taking a position of political leadership in the classroom (Katz, 1991).

In the interrogation of authority, neutrality, autonomy, and other categories of the dominant constructions of the classroom, oppositional pedagogy aims to resituate the classroom firmly within social relations, enabling students to recognize themselves as social subjects, their ideas and opinions determined by their situation within larger discourses in culture—discourses of race, class, gender, sexuality, and nationality. The outcome is in part to "put students in their place," revealing the assumptions and consequences of their positions but also revealing their place to be a contradictory one, for students are pressured to own the consequences of their positions but also see their particular positions as serving interests perhaps not entirely their own. By allowing students to recognize their situatedness, an oppositional pedagogy aims at producing students capable of engaging actively in struggles over the production of knowledge, as political subjects already implicated in those struggles—a position that goes beyond the conventional limit of having one's say included in the classroom and that has the potential to create a real democratization of knowledge both in and beyond the classroom.

Oppositional Pedagogy as Opposition

The goals of an oppositional pedagogy are fundamentally different from those understood to be the ends of pedagogical theory, which include the production of better teaching in the classroom and the development of new technologies for transmitting the existing system of education. An oppositional pedagogy aims to pressure the assumptions of the existing system—the dominant knowledges and the institutional and social arrangements derived from them—and so enable students to change their relationships to those social arrangements—ultimately to transform those social relations themselves. That the contemporary academy could potentially be a site for any kind of oppositional practice has been the focus of much debate, particularly among the left. It has been suggested that the increasing gap between radical intellectuals and mass political opposition is in large part a result of historical shifts that have worked to contain intellectuals within the academy. These arguments, which often blame intellectuals themselves for their containment or suppression (as though they have chosen this set of historical and material conditions to work under), recirculate the familiar dismissal of academia as an ivory tower and of intellectual work as mere frivolity. Such trivializations are not without real political effects. They produce a pervasive quietism by suggesting that there is always some more ideal, authentic place for action than where one already is, and they ignore the fact that academia is the site both of the reproduction of dominant interests and of their critique by oppositional ones (literally the "threat" neoconservatives currently fear). Rather than committing to a threat-free neutrality, as dominant pedagogy does, oppositional pedagogy is committed to enlarging the force of this threat. By making visible to students the political interestedness of the struggles that shape the production of knowledge and by exploring the relation of these struggles to other sites of struggle, oppositional teachers help create the possibilities for social transformation—the conditions under which critique, to paraphrase Marx, can become a material force.

References

Althusser, L. *Lenin and Philosophy and Other Essays.* New York: Monthly Review Press, 1971.
Eble, K. E. *The Craft of Teaching: A Guide to Mastering the Professor's Art.* (2nd ed.) San Francisco: Jossey-Bass, 1988.
Freire, P. *Pedagogy of the Oppressed.* (M. B. Ramos, trans.) New York: Continuum, 1970.
Glazer, N. Y. "Questioning Eclectic Practice in Curriculum Change: A Marxist Perspective." *Signs,* 1987, 12 (2), 293-304.
Hancock, L. "Teacher Comforts." *Village Voice,* July 24, 1990, p. 75.
Katz, A. "The University and Revolutionary Practice: Towards a Leninist Pedagogy." In D. Morton and M. Zavarzadeh (eds.), *Theory/Pedagogy/Politics.* Chicago: University of Illinois Press, in press.
Kimball, R. *Tenured Radicals: How Politics Has Corrupted Our Higher Education.* New York: Harper & Row, 1990.
Mandel, E. *Late Capitalism.* London: Verso, 1975.
Rosenblatt, R. "The Universities: A Bitter Attack . . ." *New York Times,* April 22, 1990, p. 36.
Ulmer, G. L. *Applied Grammatology.* Baltimore, Md.: Johns Hopkins University Press, 1985.
Walkerdine, V. "Progressive Pedagogy and Political Struggle." *Screen,* 1986, 27 (5), 54-60.
Zavarzadeh, M. "Theory as Resistance." *Rethinking Marxism,* 1989, 2 (1), 50-70.

Minette Marcroft is a graduate student in the English department at Syracuse University. As an undergraduate at the University of Utah, she worked closely with Kenneth Eble.

The community college succeeds at educating students and provides a humane environment in which to teach and to learn.

The Lower End of Higher Education: Freshmen, Sophomores, the Research University, and the Community College

Timothy R. Bywater

> The junior college, partly because higher education in its current temper does not want to deal with it and partly because the community very much wants to have it in its midst, invariably moves into the public school's orbit. Without criticizing the aims and attainments of the public school, one can say that it is organized towards the community, towards the life one has had, towards the stable world as it is. Such an orientation is precisely what higher education should not have.
> —Eble, 1966.

Kenneth Eble, although a highly respected university professor and nationally renowned scholar, saw his role mainly as that of undergraduate teacher. I find it troubling that his last years as teacher were spent in an academic environment dominated by the reactionary educational reform in vogue during the Reagan and Bush presidencies, a period in American education not exactly "kind and gentle" to American undergraduate students. Probably the most prestigious of undergraduate education's critics during these years has been the noted humanities scholar and professor, Allan Bloom (1987), codirector of the John M. Olin Center for Inquiry into the Theory and Practice of Democracy at the University of Chicago. His critique of American higher education, *The Closing of the American Mind:*

How Higher Education Has Failed Democracy and Impoverished the Souls of Today's Students, is representative of the attacks on the education establishment that have marked the Reagan-Bush years.

The Contexts of Bloom's Theory

The contrast between Bloom's and Eble's beliefs concerning undergraduate education is stark. Bloom's model perfectly reflects the economic theory that underlies the Reagan revolution. To get the country's economy moving after the Carter years, Reagan postulated that the rich should be allowed to keep more profit, creating incentives to produce more, which would result in some of the increased earnings filtering down to the working class. This trickle-down theory has always been central to the way many university professors view their teaching role and obviously is central to Bloom's thinking. It is this model that Eble deplored in much of his writing about undergraduate education.

Bloom, although he doesn't use economic jargon, regards the academic field of study as a commodity and the university professor as the capitalist entrepreneur, amassing a great storehouse of knowledge through formal research, then filtering that knowledge down to his graduate students from whom it eventually reaches the lowly undergraduate. The graduate schools at most major universities prepare their Ph.D.'s using this model. However, the trickle-down model both in economics and education has little room for the weakest members of the system. The economic model perceives the poor as somehow morally inferior since they cannot succeed in the capitalist system; therefore, they can be treated as less than human—consider, for example, the explosion in the number of homeless in major cities during the last ten years. Along similar lines, Bloom's educational model regards undergraduate freshmen and sophomores as the homeless of higher education, who if they can't cope with the system, deserve what they get: eviction.

Bloom's Versus Eble's Conception of Students

Bloom cannot hide his attitude, either condescending or contemptuous, toward students coming into his presence from the bankrupt undergraduate school system. Here is how Bloom (1987) describes "my students" to whom he dedicates his book: "Today's select students know so much less, are so cut off from the tradition, are so much slacker intellectually, that they make their predecessors look like prodigies of culture. The soil is ever thinner, and I doubt whether it can now sustain the taller growths" (p. 51). Bloom decries students' inability to read, their ignorance of the masterworks of antiquity, and their narrow interests that focus mainly on popular culture. He sees his students' lack of knowledge as a threat to Western civilization.

He objects, as most conservatives object, to the changing relationship between students and teachers, adults and children, marking the breakdown of authority that began in the midsixties. As a professor emersed in "trickle down," he obviously lost some control and power when, in the sixties, students demanded that the education system respond to their needs and begin to trickle from the bottom up. Bloom's contempt for students raised in the aftermath of the cultural revolution of the sixties and seventies is a central tenet of his thesis, no matter how elaborately he wraps that contempt in intellectual garb.

Eble, a genuinely kind and gentle man, gave undergraduate students, no matter how academically naive, admiration and respect. In his excellent books on higher education, *The Profane Comedy* (1963), *The Perfect Education* (1966), *Professors as Teachers* (1972), and *The Craft of Teaching* (1988), Eble both examined the failure of the university professor to teach undergraduates effectively and suggested many ways to improve the situation. In *The Perfect Education* he succinctly pointed out the university's major deficiency as a place to teach and to learn—its failure to "foster the relationship between the single student and the single teacher" (p. 156). That goal, according to Eble, is important beyond all others. In another place he gives this advice to the university professor trying to teach undergraduate students: "For a great variety of students, in a country still various and full in its physical surroundings, academic life must seek to match the geography. It must be less housebound. It must be as respectful of the ground the scholar walks as the upper elevations he would occupy. It must pose real trips to places of the mind and have the kinds of teachers who can be good companions for the road."

Eble's Approach to Teaching

Eble's approach is the antithesis of the contemptuous attitude that damns not only Bloom's book but much that is going on at the research university under the title of teaching. A battle for human lives is being fought, not some intellectual battle of the books. At present the Ebles are losing. What makes matters worse is that the excellent teaching that does take place at the research university rarely gets to the students who will benefit the most from it: freshmen and sophomores. They are often taught by teaching assistants (TAs), by the burned-out, or by young assistant professors on the make, who often see it as their duty to weed out the unprepared. The sixties revolution pushed the research university to move away from bigness for its own sake, to reallocate resources from the all-powerful graduate school to undergraduate teaching, to reduce publishing pressure for the research-driven assistant professor, to provide some dignity for the freshman and sophomore student often treated as a cipher in the university bureaucracy. Eble celebrated those changes and pushed for more, but the years of change were short lived. Today, those who see education—students and curriculum—as a commodity are firmly in control. They become the directors of prestigious humanities centers, they publish the books and articles, they appear on the talk shows. Bloom, of course, has played the game.

If the sixties ideal—Eble's teacher as a "companion for the road"—is ever to become a reality, it must happen somewhere outside of Bloom's research university. Thus, the final hope to provide a favorable academic environment for nurturing the Eble ideal may lie in the two-year community college system.

The Community College and Its Strengths

After finishing my Ph.D. with Eble as my major adviser, I entered a tight job market and spent several years in temporary appointments, teaching English at the university level. My first tenure-track appointment came at a small community college, at first an unsatisfactory place to teach for someone coming from the research university atmosphere and mind-set. And yet something about the community college system seemed tailor-made for me, since I had been taught the significance of the individual student by Eble's example. The community college began to look like the place to foster the "perfect" undergraduate education.

From my experience as a teacher and administrator at the community college level for the last seven years, I can see more clearly now its strengths as a teaching institution when compared with the research university. These strengths include (1) colleague interaction across the curriculum; (2) teaching atmosphere; (3) professional development, research, and scholarly publishing opportunities removed from university pressure; and (4) influence of both teachers and administrators on the student and on the institution.

Collegiality at the Community College. The one unequivocal statement I can make concerning the academic environment at the community college is that in this environment I have had a unique opportunity to interact with colleagues from a variety of academic disciplines. Symbolic of this opportunity would have to be the lunchroom discussions in my community college's liberal arts building. I had always considered the teacher's lunchroom to be a high school invention, so when I was invited to eat lunch with the faculty in our building, I was skeptical. Little did I realize that I was being invited to one of the most intellectually stimulating ongoing discussions that I have ever been involved in on any academic level. At the universities where I taught, I would occasionally go to lunch with my colleagues. But at this community college's informal colloquium, every day there will be an eclectic sampling of thought from various humanities and social science disciplines, including psychology, sociology, economics, political science, history, British literature, film study, American literature, humanities, composition, German—with an occasional visit from the president of the college.

These lunchroom discussions provide a forum for exploring ideas that run the gamut in these disciplines and can range to all topics, including arguments concerning the latest National Basketball Association or National Football League playoffs. At first, I was a reticent participant in these sessions; now they affect me like a drug—I need a daily fix. Missing from our division is the internecine warfare that often occurs in large university departments. Naturally, differences of opinion arise, as they will, when an argument develops between a Milton Freedman economist and a Jessie Jackson supporter. But seldom do these differences go beyond intellectual argument that is stimulating and interesting and not born of jealousy or mistrust. I believe that the breakdown of departmental barriers that takes place at the community college plays a major role in creating a more open, relaxed atmosphere in which to interact with colleagues.

It was, in my opinion, the lunchroom discussions that initiated our division's interdisciplinary humanities courses: "Technology, Growth and the Environment," "Utopias," and "Death and Dying." These courses, made possible by a National Endowment for the Humanities grant, are team-taught by our lunchroom faculty: a sociologist and a British literature specialist, a political scientist and an American literature expert, and an economist and a Shakespeare scholar. The courses represent the variety that we can offer in our division and the variety available to students in the community college system. With teaching emphasis placed on the first two college years, freshmen and sophomores are immediately exposed to an exciting curriculum developed and taught by the permanent faculty—not a curriculum developed by a graduate school director, steeped in the latest theory, and taught by teaching assistants or in arena-sized classrooms. A look at our community college catalogue indicates that our offerings are as diverse and interesting as one will find at the freshman and sophomore level at many four-year colleges or universities.

Teaching Atmosphere. Although part of our mission involves articulating transfer courses with four-year schools, we are also able, because of our manageable size and acute sensitivity to student needs, to experiment with courses designed specifically for our student population. The students are a mixture of the finest, most academically committed to the poorest, least prepared. I'm still stunned at the lack of engagement of some of them and by their failure to appreciate the wonderful educational opportunity that the community college offers. But because of the open admission policy, all students have the chance to be exposed to the challenges of higher education, fitted to their academic skills. This flexibility represents a genuine example of the democratic ideal in action. The staff and the administration are committed to this ideal and are continually searching for innovative ways to reach all students.

Over the last few years, we have created a developmental program for students not prepared to enter freshman-level courses. Recently, we received an $1.5 million donation to construct a building to house this program. Last year we began to develop an honors program, which all college divisions have strongly supported. The core of this program is based on a series of faculty training seminars led by master teachers from across the country. Faculty members from every discipline on campus come together during several one-week sessions spaced throughout the academic year and during the summer to read literary and philosophical works and to discuss the major issues raised by those works that cut across departmental boundaries. These faculty members will then team-teach honors courses focused on the ideas generated by the seminars. The seminars have enabled faculty members from across campus to get to know and appreciate each other's ideas. From my experience in academia, these seminars, breaking down department and division barriers, would have been literally impossible in the research university setting.

Opportunities for Faculty Development. Although the focus at the community college is on teaching, faculty development and scholarship are not slighted. In our division, all faculty members are working to enhance their academic and scholarly expertise. In the last two years, our humanities and social science faculty have been granted two Fulbright fellowships, one Ph.D. from Oxford University, and many courses completed beyond the master's level, with at least four professors at various stages of work toward the Ph.D. Other divisions are equally active.

Publishing and grant writing, although not stressed, are also enthusiastically supported by the college administration. Members of our faculty have authored and published poetry, short stories, novels, scholarly papers, textbooks, and have received national grants. Several of our faculty use their expertise to consult in areas related to their academic fields. Although money is extremely tight, every year most members of our division have been able to attend conferences dealing with their academic interests.

In my case, working at a community college has made my scholarship and writing possible. I have had strong support for my research projects from everyone at the college. I have a clear sense that my colleagues want me to succeed. They encourage me by offering to proofread my articles, to brainstorm my ideas, and to let me known when I'm off target. I am not threatened by their criticism. I'm not sure why, but I guess it's because they are fellow teachers, not scholarly competitors. The overt publish-or-perish pressure and cutthroat competition often connected with university scholarship are absent here. At the community college, scholarly pursuit is placed in proper perspective; the reason that we're here is simple: to teach and to learn. Our scholarship and research are grounded in those goals.

Influence of Teachers and Administrators. Recently, while accepting a distinguished service award, a community college faculty member nearing retirement had this to say about his role at the college: "I could have never had the opportunity to be so involved and to do the things I've done anyplace else but here." I agree and would add that what I do (and what all of us at community colleges do) has an immediate impact on students, students who are often lost in the research shuffle at big universities. The community college student can rely on us for academic and personal guidance during the crucial first two years of college, arguably the most important years in a student's academic life.

At the community college, I have many more opportunities to influence the community and our students than I believe I would have had at a research institution. One year, for example, I thought it would be a good idea if our students had the chance to hear guest speakers with a variety of points of view. As a result, I was put in charge of a speaker's forum, which during the year brought several nationally prominent speakers, including Kenneth Eble, to the campus. The community college academic environment provides each faculty member with the chance to make a difference.

Pitfalls of the Community College

Although the community college is in an ideal position to influence undergraduate teaching positively, problems often intervene. I have attempted to point out the strengths of the community college compared with the research university, but there are also weaknesses. As an English teacher, I have been made acutely aware that the state is no more receptive to the aims of student-centered teaching as a primary mission than the research university is. Like the research university, the state is always concerned with the bottom line. At the mercy of state legislatures, community colleges sell out to the business community. Our mission often becomes vocational education, and the primary motivation for teaching then becomes vocational training. Even the humanities must justify their existence in terms of practical application. The state, following the Reagan (and Bloom) model, attempts to turn the community college curriculum into a commodity.

The other impediment to quality undergraduate education at the community college is, as the name "community" implies, the fact that academic concerns are closely tied to community interests and pressure. Eble (1966) was aware of this danger and wrote of it in *The Perfect Education*. He correctly perceived that the community college had been assigned the role of educating freshmen and sophomores by default, "partly because higher education in its current temper does not want to deal with it and partly because the community very much wants to have it in its midst" (p. 129). As a result, according to Eble, the community college "invariably moves into the public school's orbit" (p. 129). Eble saw this as an eminent threat to higher education, for it can mean that the community college functions not as a college at all but as a glorified high school.

From my experience, I can attest to the fact that these dangers are real. Leadership with the expressed goal of turning the community colleges into centers of superior undergraduate teaching and learning is lacking. The presidents of community colleges usually receive their training at research universities, often in advanced business or in graduate school programs. They believe their training to be the only legitimate academic model. For example, the president of the college where I teach, a former director of an honors program at a state university, is pressuring faculty to teach arena-sized classes, no doubt with the blessing of the state board of regents. Since the research university model is the only one he has known, he has not yet come to grips with the potential of the community college to do a better job of educating freshmen and sophomores than can be done at the research university.

Conclusion

The academic environment at the community college, because of these problems, does not get the attention or credit it deserves for what it does well; however, the fact that the research university has abdicated its teaching role places the community college in a better position to lead the way to quality education for freshmen and sophomores. If the community college assumes this role, then the research university, the state legislature, and the business community may come to understand the real goal of the perfect education, as embodied by the community college and as eloquently described by Eble (1966) in his conclusion to *The Perfect Education:*

> Education cannot change the ultimate facts of decline and death, but it can plunge one into life and keep one there: It can provide that overarching life of a people, a community, a world that was going on before the individual came onto the scene and that will continue on unchecked after he departs. . . . By such means we come to see the world feelingly and not alone. Our joys are more intense for being shared. Our sorrows are less destructive for our knowing universal sorrow. Our pride is chastened by an awareness of our betters. Our fears of death fade before the commonness of the occurrence. All humanity argues against our marching blindly toward death. Education, above all, gives value to life. The more we see on the way, the more we feel, the more we ponder over the journey, the more we ask of education, and the more it can give [pp. 214–215].

References

Bloom, A. *The Closing of the American Mind: How Higher Education Has Failed Democracy and Impoverished the Souls of Today's Students.* New York: Simon & Schuster, 1987.
Eble, K. E. *The Profane Comedy.* New York: Macmillan, 1963.
Eble, K. E. *The Perfect Education: Growing Up in Utopia.* New York: Macmillan, 1966.
Eble, K. E. *Professors as Teachers.* San Francisco: Jossey-Bass, 1972.
Eble, K. E. *The Craft of Teaching: A Guide to Mastering the Professor's Art.* (2nd ed.) San Francisco: Jossey-Bass, 1988.

Timothy R. Bywater is dean of the division of humanities and social sciences at Dixie College in St. George, Utah.

The computer may always be with us, but in spite of its manifold usefulness, there is no consistent objective evidence showing that it can help students become better writers.

What Good Are Computers in the Writing Classroom?

Michael Dobberstein

> Technology does not promise to revolutionize learning and teaching. At most, it offers a series of changes which have already modified the behavior of students within learning situations and which have altered in various ways the learning situation.
> —Eble, 1972.

The computer is no longer the coming thing. It has arrived; it is as certain a part of our professional lives as committee meetings, grading papers, debates about writing pedagogy, and the pursuit of tenure. Even though we may not agree on just what all the fuss is about, the computer has become a presence in the college curriculum that few of us can avoid (Smallen, 1989).

For teachers of writing, its presence is especially pressing. More than our colleagues who teach traditional literary subjects, we flatter ourselves that we prepare our students for the world of work, a world whose computer purchases have increased at a rate of 24 percent a year while investment in other kinds of business equipment has actually gone down (Baily, 1989).

Thus, many of us have installed computers in our classes, if only to give our students the opportunity to work with machines that they will have to use after graduation. More important, we are under the impression that using computers will help our students become better writers (Munter, 1986), happier writers (Pearson, 1987), or at least neater writers (Barbour, 1988). Since many of us believe that revision is the key to good writing, we see word processing on the computer as a breakthrough technology that improves student writing because it allows revision with incredible ease.

Professional writers attest to how ease of revision facilitates the creation of texts (Lutz, 1987), and many of us who have taken up word processing would not readily go back to the typewriter or to pen and paper. But these are separate issues entirely from whether or not word processing actually can improve writing. However we may cherish the belief that this technology strengthens student writing (or anyone else's, for that matter), we must ask ourselves what evidence exists that justifies our faith.

Is there proof, in other words, that students become better writers through the use of word processing in the classroom? Since the early 1980s, a growing number of studies have tried to answer this question objectively, though with mixed results. While data exist that suggest that word processing may help students improve their writing, it is by no means certain that word processing alone can enhance writing skills. If we who teach writing are to keep this technology in perspective, we need to take a close look at some of these studies.

Evaluating Word Processing in the Classroom

Making sense of this body of research is not an easy task. As Hawisher (1986) points out in an early review, many studies seeking to assess the influence of word processing on student writing differ widely in "research design, in method of data collection, in variables examined, and in the analysis of data" (p. 6). Of the twenty-four research projects she evaluates, Hawisher notes a mixture of experimental, ethnographic, and exploratory studies, case studies, and surveys. In addition, samples range in size from two to ninety-six subjects and include grade school students, college freshmen, journalists, and graduate students.

Because of these differences, generalizations about results are difficult to make. Hawisher tentatively concludes that most of those studied liked using the computer to write and that they perceived word processing as having a positive influence on their writing. But taken as a whole, the studies examined by Hawisher (1986) are not compatible enough in design to show that word processing can actually improve writing skills.

The Importance of Experimental Design. In showing whether or not word processing in writing classes makes college students better writers, studies must go beyond merely "emphasizing students, their writing, and computers" (Hawisher, 1986, p. 6). Consistency of research design is particularly helpful, and the studies that have the most to tell us about the effect of word processing on student writing skills are experimental in design. In these studies, the writing performance of students using word processing is compared to that of students in control groups who received the same writing instruction but did not use word processing. This comparative method has long been recognized as the most effective way of determining the influence of an instructional method on students (Jaeger, 1983).

A number of experimental studies exist that examine the effects of word processing on the writing quality of grade school, high school, and college students. Though some of these studies make impressive claims for the success of word processing in making students better writers, it is important to note that this body of research is inconsistent in showing that word processing can improve student writing.

A Comparison of Experimental Studies. Results of experimental studies are not only inconsistent as a whole, they are inconsistent within the student groups examined. For instance, though Kaplan's (1986) study of fifth graders showed that word processing improved holistic writing scores, Woolley (1985) found that word processing had no significant effect on the writing quality of the fifth graders that he examined. Duling (1985) found that while ninth graders revised more frequently using word processors, overall writing quality was unaffected; yet Pivarnik (1985) concluded that eleventh graders trained in word processing wrote better essays than eleventh graders who wrote with pen and paper.

Studies focusing on college students show the same equivocal results. Bernhardt, Wojahn, and Edwards (1988); Etchison (1985); Sommers (1985); Teichman and Poris (1985); Vockell and Schwartz (1988); and Weiss (1988) all claim significant success in showing that using word processing can improve the writing of college students. However, Varner and Grogg (1988) and Hawisher (1987) conclude that word processing has little effect on the quality of college student writing.

The studies claiming positive results in college classrooms are hard to ignore. The number of them (six) is impressive, and they share many important characteristics: Though some had more than one objective, all specifically examined the effect of word processing on writing quality; all (except for Weiss, 1988) used college freshmen as subjects; all (again except for Weiss, 1988) compared data collected from pre- and postinstruction writing samples; all evaluated data "blindly" (that is, raters did not know if essays were written by students in the control or computer groups); and ratings of all studies showed a high degree of reliability.

Yet differences among these studies in sample size and method of evaluation should be noted. Though three used large samples of 100 or more students (Bernhardt, Wojahn, and Edwards, 1988; Etchison, 1985; Teichman and Poris, 1985), Vockell and Schwartz (1988), Weiss (1988), and Sommers (1985) used smaller samples. And while Vockell and Schwartz used the Diedrich scale to evaluate writing samples, the others used a variety of criteria, including a holistic score, to measure writing ability. Weiss (1988), whose subjects were juniors and seniors instead of freshmen, compared scores on class assignments rather than using pre- and postinstruction essays to evaluate improvement.

Three of these five experimental studies (Bernhardt, Wojahn, and Edwards, 1988; Etchison, 1985; Teichman and Poris, 1985) are the most directly comparable in sample size, method of evaluation, and variables studied. These studies analyzed writing performance for instructor effect as well as for word-processing effect. The results, aside from indicating that word processing had a positive effect on student writing, are not entirely consistent. In addition, close examination of two of these studies reveals that even positive results may be questionable.

Bernhardt, Wojahn, and Edwards (1988) found that the 146 students who had used computers in a freshman composition course were able to improve their writing through revision significantly more than the 194 students who had had the same writing instruction but had not used computers. However, analysis of the data showed that instructors had a strong effect on student performance, indicating that the quality of teaching may have been at least partly responsible for the writing improvements.

In comparing pre- and postinstruction writing samples (pretests and posttests) from fifty computer students and fifty regular students, Etchison (1985) concluded that the computer students made a gain in holistic writing quality of more than five times that of the regular students and that instructors had no significant effect on student performance. However, the computer students' mean pretest scores were nearly two points lower than the regular students' pretest scores, and as Hawisher (1986) notes, Etchison's results do not take into account the possibility of regression. That is, in studies that depend on comparing preinstruction and postinstruction tests, lower-scoring groups almost always improve, while higher-scoring groups tend to "fall back" (Freedman, Pisani, and Purves, 1978, p. 159), rendering a large spread between the two groups' mean posttest scores questionable.

The 1985 study of Teichman and Poris, extending over two years and involving 320 students, claims that the use of word processing "significantly enhanced" student writing (p. 1) and that instructors had no meaningful effect on writing performance. However, Teichman and Poris are unclear about how much computer students' writing improved compared to regular students, and as with the Etchison study, regression was apparently not taken into account. In other words, pre- to posttest gains for computer students were possibly significant at least partly because that group had lower pretest scores than the control group.

The positive results of the remaining three studies—Sommers (1985), Vockell and Schwartz (1988), and Weiss (1988)—must also be qualified. None of these three analyzes its data for instructor effect, though Weiss (1988) acknowledges the importance of such an effect when he points out that in his study "teacher-researcher bias favoring the computer group . . . cannot be ruled out" (p. 151). And though Sommers (1985) reports statistically significant improvement in computer students' writing ability compared to that of noncomputer students, she admits that "the improvement is small and perhaps undistinguished in view of the instructional effort made" (p. 22).

Interestingly, results from the two studies that examine business writing students instead of freshmen (Weiss, 1988; Varner and Grogg, 1988) are contradictory. Weiss, in comparing assignments from sixty-two business and technical writing students, concluded that those in the computer group wrote significantly better essays than their noncomputer counterparts. In studying data from eighty-eight upper-division business writing students, Varner and Grogg found that those in the computer group spent less time on their assignments than noncomputer students. However, computer students showed no gains in writing improvement compared to noncomputer students.

Conclusion

Though their study of microcomputers in the business writing classroom showed that word processing had little effect on the quality of student writing, Varner and Grogg (1988) quote Steven Jobs approvingly when he proclaims that the personal computer is "the finest tool that the finest tool builders who have ever lived on the earth have built" (p. 69). But whatever the personal computer's manifold virtues may be as an aid in the creation of text, the calculation of spreadsheets, the collection of data, and the design of publications or as a method for communication, the evidence that it can improve student writing is far from conclusive.

There is evidence that students like using computers to write, and this may be important. Hawisher's (1986) tentative conclusion that students generally react favorably to writing with a word processor is consistent with the findings of later surveys (Beck and Stibravy, 1986; Bernhardt, Wojahn, and Edwards, 1988; Dalton and Hannafin, 1987). An implication of such a positive attitude may be that the incorporation of the computer into the writing syllabus will make the learning of writing a better experience for some students, and this may provide motivation for those students to become better writers.

Significantly, some students seem to like the computer more than others. Bernhardt, Wojahn, and Edwards (1988) found that some students "take ownership of the computer" (p. 22), developing useful revision strategies, while others do not. And in her second review of studies in word processing, Hawisher (1988) concludes that writers' predispositions to revise or not may have more effect on writing performance than the computer. These findings suggest that writers who understand the importance of revision may find the computer a more useful tool than those who do not.

But if our quest is for better ways to teach writing, we may have to look no further than ourselves. Bernhardt, Wojahn, and Edwards (1988), while concluding that the computer can improve student revising skills, state flatly that "if our goal were simply improved student writing, we would probably get better results from choosing talented teachers or from training our teachers than from introducing computers into the classroom. . . . Teachers, not machines, have the strongest effect on student writing improvement" (pp. 22-23).

Even if Bernhardt, Wojahn, and Edwards are wrong about the importance of instructor effect on student writing performance, we must ask not only whether but *how much* computers can improve student writing. This question addresses the allocation of resources: Even if computers alone can improve writing quality, what degree of improvement is necessary to justify the enormous expense and effort of installing and maintaining computers in the classroom? Experimental studies cannot answer this; they can only help us refine our judgment about the significance of possible writing improvement.

Finally, we cannot ignore the ambiguous impact of computers outside the university. The promise of the "computer revolution"—which saw millions of personal computers installed in business offices—was that computers would increase the productivity of office workers, and we can now see that this has not happened. While some companies have seen gains in white-collar productivity because of computers, generally such productivity has remained flat since the 1960s (Bowen, 1986). In fact, productivity growth in the last decade has slowed, though business invested billions of dollars in computer hardware and software throughout the 1980s (Baily, 1989).

The reasons for this are hard to pin down. Baily suggests that personal computers, especially, may be underused, at least in part because learning how to use them effectively is harder than anyone thought. Another possibility is that we have simply expected more of the computer than it can actually provide. We may be expecting far too much if we believe that it can improve writing skills.

References

Baily, M. N. "Great Expectations: PCs and Productivity." *PC Computing,* April 1989, pp. 137-141.
Barbour, D. H. "The Word-Processing Lab in the Business Writing Course." *Bulletin of the Association for Business Communication,* 1988, *51* (3), 19-20.
Beck, C. E., and Stibravy, J. A. "The Effect of Word Processors on Writing Quality." *Technical Communication,* Second Quarter 1986, pp. 84-87.
Bernhardt, S., Wojahn, P., and Edwards, P. "Teaching College Composition with Computers: A Program Evaluation Study." 1988. (ED 295 191)
Bowen, W. "The Puny Payoff from Office Computers." *Fortune,* May 1986, pp. 20-24.
Dalton, D. W., and Hannafin, M. J. "The Effects of Word Processing on Written Composition." *Journal of Educational Research,* 1987, *80,* 338-342.
Duling, R. A. "Word Processors and Student Writing: A Study of Their Impact on Revision, Fluency, and Quality of Writing." *Dissertation Abstracts International,* 1985, *46* (7), 1823A.

Eble, K. E. *Professors as Teachers*. San Francisco: Jossey-Bass, 1972.
Etchison, C. "A Comparative Study of the Quality and Syntax of Compositions by First-Year College Writers Using Handwriting and Word Processing." 1985. (ED 282 215)
Freedman, D., Pisani, R., and Purves, R. *Statistics*. New York: Norton, 1978.
Hawisher, G. E. "Studies in Word Processing." *Computers and Composition*, 1986, 4 (1), 6-31.
Hawisher, G. E. "The Effects of Word Processing on the Revision Strategies of College Freshmen." *Research in the Teaching of English*, 1987, 21, 145-159.
Hawisher, G. E. "Research in Computers and Writing: Findings and Implications." 1988. (ED 293 140)
Jaeger, R. M. *Statistics: A Spectator Sport*. Newbury Park, Calif.: Sage, 1983.
Kaplan, H. "Computers and Composition: Improving Students' Written Performance." *Dissertation Abstracts International*, 1986, 47 (3), 76A.
Lutz, J. A. "A Study of Professional and Experienced Writers Revising and Editing at the Computer and with Pen and Paper." *Research in the Teaching of English*, 1987, 21, 398-421.
Munter, M. "Using the Computer in Business Communication Courses." *Journal of Business Communication*, 1986, 23 (1), 31-42.
Pearson, P. "Turning on to Word Processing." *Bulletin of the Association for Business Communication*, 1987, 50 (2), 19-23.
Pivarnik, B. A. "The Effect of Training in Word Processing on the Writing Quality of Eleventh-Grade Students." *Dissertation Abstracts International*, 1985, 46 (7), 1827A.
Smallen, D. L. "Infusing Computing into the Curriculum: Challenges for the Next Decade." *Academic Computing*, April 1989, pp. 8-10.
Sommers, E. "The Effects of Word Processing and Writing Instruction on the Writing Processes and Products of College Writers." 1985. (ED 269 762)
Teichman, M., and Poris, M. "Word Processing in the Classroom: Its Effects on Freshman Writers." 1985. (ED 276 062)
Varner, I. I., and Grogg, P. M. "Microcomputers and the Writing Process." *Journal of Business Communication*, 1988, 25 (3), 69-78.
Vockell, E. L., and Schwartz, E. "Microcomputers to Teach English Composition." *Collegiate Microcomputer*, 1988, 6 (2), 148-154.
Weiss, T. "The Effect of the Computer on Student Writing." *Technical Communication*, Second Quarter 1988, pp. 150-152.
Woolley, W. C. "The Effects of Word Processing on the Writing of Selected Fifth-Grade Students." *Dissertation Abstracts International*, 1985, 47 (1), 82A.

Michael Dobberstein is assistant professor of English at Purdue University, Calumet, in Hammond, Indiana, where he teaches a variety of writing courses.

Scholarly work, the best way for college teachers to keep vitalized, can be assessed as effectively as traditional research activities.

Encouraging and Evaluating Scholarship for the College Teacher

Paul A. Lacey

> Research should not be the single standard to which all activities outside the classroom relate. *Search* might be offered as a word which embraces more of the kinds of discoveries to be expected of higher learning.
>
> —Eble, 1972.

Samuel Johnson once said that people more often need to be reminded of what they already know than instructed in what they do not know. Anyone trying to write about improving the quality of teaching and of professional life in higher education must feel the weight, if not the comfort, of that observation. To reread Kenneth Eble's (1983, 1988) writing on teaching and faculty development is to recognize how much of the humane good sense of *The Aims of College Teaching* and *The Craft of Teaching* and much else comes as a carefully argued, experience- and research-based reminder of what we already know but neglect or ignore in practice. His example gives me warrant for writing a chapter that is also more of a reminder than new information. It takes its beginnings from two other of my works (1988, 1990), an essay on "Faculty Development and the Future of College Teaching" and one arguing that what we know about our work as college teachers shows us how future college teachers can be better prepared for their work. In the latter essay I assert that what is required of all but the small number of faculty at research institutions is not what is usually described as research leading to publication, work expected to make original contributions and additions to the body of knowledge. Instead, it is appropriate to our work and our own inclinations as teachers that our writing and other professional activities should be *scholarship* (whether it results in research publication or not), using that term as Boyer (1988) does. I also argue that such work can keep us vitalized as teachers and practitioners of our disciplines and that the fruits of such work can be assessed effectively for contract renewal, tenure and promotion judgments, and developmental purposes.

First, a grim reminder: "Standard comments about 'The American Professor' as one who engages in both teaching and research are false: Nearly all members of the professoriate teach, but only a minority are significantly involved in research" (Clark, 1987). Not only do we teach most of the time but the latest Carnegie Foundation (1989) survey reports that 71 percent of the 5,000 faculty surveyed from all levels of higher education report that they lean toward or are primarily interested in teaching, and 62 percent agree that teaching effectiveness should be the primary criterion for the promotion of faculty. Yet 54 percent believe it is difficult to get tenure in their departments without publishing, and 57 percent say that the number of publications is fairly to very important for gaining tenure. In addition, 35 percent say that the pressure to publish reduces the quality of teaching at their institution, and 68 percent agree that their institution needs better ways, besides publications, to evaluate the scholarly performance of faculty.

These faculty perceptions pose afresh three interrelated questions: (1) What can be said about the relationship of research and scholarship to undergraduate teaching? (2) What are the criteria for deciding what will be accepted as research or scholarship? (3) How can such work best be evaluated?

The Relationship of Research and Scholarship to Teaching

Conventional thought holds that faculty must be regularly involved in disciplinary research leading to publication, preferably in refereed journals deemed of high quality, as a primary means of staying current in their disciplines and of modeling what learning is. When colleagues concerned about such research ask whether anyone can teach writing who is not regularly writing or whether a scientist can teach science without being engaged in scientific research, their questions are neither trivial nor rhetorical. When they are phrased this way, in fact, the questions urge a necessary connection between teaching and traditional forms of research (*not* scholarship).

The answers provided by research into the matter are anything but categorical, however. A review in *The Teaching Professor* ("Research Focus," 1989) that digested Kenneth Feldman's (1987) meta-analysis of forty-four studies, twenty-nine of them examining correlations between teaching and research, reports the following: "On the whole, scholarly accomplishment or research productivity of college and university faculty is only slightly associated with teaching proficiency" (p. 7), but "productivity in research and scholarship does not seem to detract from being an effective teacher" (p. 8). Feldman found no evidence for the claim that time spent on research detracts from instructional effectiveness. He did find small positive associations between research productivity and knowledge of the subject, intellectual expansiveness, and organization and clarity of course objectives and requirements, but he also found "with some consistency across studies, supportiveness, tolerance, and warmth . . . were associated inversely with research productivity but positively with teaching effectiveness" (p. 8).

Feldman offers tentative conclusions with many warnings about the differences in the studies and the limits of meta-analysis. We may add that in the absence of clear definitions of what constituted research or scholarship, it is not possible to make firm judgments about some possible relationships between those activities and teaching. What Feldman confirms is that we cannot assert the presence or absence of links between teaching and research or scholarly activities simply on the basis of our ideological stand.

What we can do, then, is to consider what kinds of links exist between scholarly activities (a term I will use temporarily to dodge the disjunction between research and scholarship) and the teaching of undergraduates. Here we are helped by several studies of such activities in faculty development programs. From their study of a variety of programs supported by the Bush Foundation, Eble and McKeachie (1985) concluded that in the small, struggling colleges, the best effect of scholarly work on teaching would be applied scholarship—that is, keeping up with developments in the discipline in order to teach adequately. They also conclude that "highly specialized research in a general-purpose college is not likely to have a very good fit with the actualities of teaching" (pp. 132–133).

Clark (1987) suggests that scholarship and research must be defined in relation both to the mission of the institution and to the goals of the individual. So, for example, he makes a distinction between big science and little science:

> Small college research is less formally organized, with few, if any, research assistants and no "post-docs" to compose a research team. It is, therefore, individually more flexible. It is also typically more "horizontal" than research in the university, more often spread across neighboring subfields and even across disciplines [p. 79].

Such work engages undergraduates in genuine scientific inquiry, rather than in cookbook lab work, but the focus will typically be broader on projects designed to illustrate scientific work rather than to solve a problem. Such projects make small contributions to the body of knowledge but large contributions to the education of scientists. They are what I would define as scholarship, rather than research.

A professor in the Clark (1987) study clarifies a distinction between research and scholarship in the humanities: Scholarship "consists primarily of control of primary materials," he contends, while research is "essentially devoted to finding out something new about your topic or your author or field" (p. 92). Scholarship is more likely than research to be connected with teaching, he contends, in the humanities.

This is the kind of distinction Boyer (1988) makes when he says that every college teacher should be a first-rate scholar, though only a smaller number will be researchers working on the growing edge of a discipline or "vertically" in a tightly focused research project. Boyer also insists that such scholarly activities should be evaluated by peers in order to assess the teacher's professional growth.

A variety of scholarly activities might serve the purposes of maintaining a teacher's professional competence and enhancing his or her teaching. Boyer suggests (apart from publishing books, monographs, or journal articles) writing textbooks, participating in conferences, developing new approaches to instruction, and becoming more effective in the classroom. Weaver (1986) makes several concrete suggestions for scholarly writing that are especially compatible with the work lives of college teachers: book reviews, the review article that synthesizes and critically reinterprets research results, and articles about teaching itself. In order to design a syllabus, Weaver argues, the teacher must frame the central questions of the subject, select readings, establish rules of evidence, develop and examine interpretations that give meaning to the subject, and help students learn how to master the material and how to make their own fruitful connections between interpretations of the material. Such work requires continual reflection on the teaching and learning process, and thus the kind of writing that Weaver suggests is not only more feasible than original research but also "better complements the process of syllabus and lecture preparation" (p. 52).

Problems of Defining Acceptable Research and Scholarship

Writing on performance appraisal methods for faculty, Blackburn and Pitney (1988) argue that performance appraisal works well for people engaged in traditional research; the peer review process—critiquing and revising before publication—is accepted by both faculty and administrators as an appropriate means of appraisal. The problem with accepted practice, however, "is that it affects only a small share of the professoriate. . . . Scholarship, or creative work, for the vast majority of the faculty is frequently not subject to peer review.... There is a long list of creative activities that most colleges value and need but seldom appraise" (pp. 27-28).

The issue is not that such activities are not amenable to appraisal but that they have been excluded from consideration, perhaps through inadvertence but more likely deliberately. In his survey of 274 institutions, Weaver (1986) found that respondents from research universities and liberal arts colleges "were the most definite about not encouraging faculty to write and publish about their teaching" (p. 51). Again, the problem is not that writing about teaching and a number of other activities that keep teachers intellectually alive and effective in the classroom are not being done and done well; it is that they are excluded from consideration by definition. Many teachers have experienced that publishing a textbook, even one that is a leader in its field, will not count for tenure or promotion and may even be held against them in evaluations of scholarship. Only disciplinary research published in refereed journals is acceptable as proof of professional activity.

It is possible that all those faculty members are mistaken who believe that publications are overvalued as evidence of scholarly activity and who believe that publications are only counted, not qualitatively measured, at their institutions. But there are some independent confirmations of these perceptions. Soderberg (1985), citing studies by Centra (1979) and Gastron, Lantz, and Snyder (1975), asserts that despite the claim that research quality is valued, the number of publications is what gets rewarded. Of sixteen criteria that might be used to evaluate research, number of articles in quality journals was ranked first by department heads of 134 higher education institutions.

At first glance, requiring publications in refereed journals would appear to be a sensible way to get objective peer assessments reflecting high academic standards. But every now and then someone tries an experiment that shakes our faith in that review process. Ceci and Young (1982) made one such test, resubmitting thirteen previously published articles that had been written by researchers from prestigious institutions, substituting names of researchers from less prestigious institutions. Three essays were recognized; nine of the remaining ten articles were summarily rejected by twenty different peer evaluators, without so much as a suggestion that rewriting might help any of the articles to become acceptable.

In a similar test of the experts—in this case publishers and editors—Doris Lessing submitted new works of her own under a pseudonym; all the works were rejected. In a test tried on American publishers, several contemporary literary classics were resubmitted "over the transom" with different names attached. Few of the works were recognized, and none of the unrecognized got a nibble for publication.

We should not let such experiments tempt us too far into satire. It is enough to point out the danger of overdependence on experts to do evaluations for us. In particular, letting independent peer review for quality journals assess written work has its risks. Such peer reviews may be detached, but they may be neither objective nor unbiased. The vast number of journals now being published presents serious problems of quality control, and it does not follow that the best things will invariably appear in what particular schools within the discipline consider the best journals or that all referees are dependable judges of what they read.

Evaluation of Scholarship and Research

In focusing so heavily on what is usually called "research productivity," we are asking the wrong questions and assessing for the wrong things. Here I must confess a bias. During my college summers, I worked in a factory; there I discovered that productivity meant piecework and that I earned most per hour when the tasks were most mindless. I have been suspicious of productivity tests ever since. Everyone hopes to be a productive human being, but something happens when we shift the emphasis in education to an industrial model and begin talking about productivity.

On many counts, the present ways in which higher education evaluates both research and scholarship are either inadequate or counterproductive. They do not tell us what we need to know. Many activities that are valuable for our institutions are excluded from consideration and receive no professional review. Blackburn and Pitney (1988) assert "the generally accepted meaning of scholarship today, namely publications, differs dramatically across disciplines in the kinds of products and their rate of output" (p. 31). Even within disciplines, great variation is the rule, and the scholarly and creative work of the majority of professors is diffuse. "It is not that most are unscholarly; rather, they present their creative efforts in a wide variety of ways, almost none of which possess a standard with which its quality can be judged or at any rate can be advanced as 'normal'" (p. 31).

In my own college, faculty are not required to publish in order to receive tenure or promotion. Teaching is the most important of four criteria, and we address the issues of professional vitality under the heading "quality of mind." We examine teaching effectiveness and quality of mind in contract renewal, tenure, and the five-year posttenure reviews. Under that heading we have a chance to consider whether a faculty member continues to grow intellectually and professionally, is stimulated by teaching and by students, stays engaged and up to date with the field, and reaches out to connect with other disciplines.

There is nothing magic about the term *quality of mind*, but I suggest that asking the questions it enfolds will lead to considering a much wider variety of materials and activities for the answers. We would examine intellectual activities that have outcomes in teaching, looking especially for evidences of breadth and connectedness, raising value questions in relation to our discipline, and encouraging cooperation in learning, as Eble (1983) suggested. Materials that in a more rigid system of classification would be considered only under assessment of teaching—syllabi, choice of readings, lectures, assignments, methods of grading—can equally well be considered as evidence of the faculty member's quality of mind. Does the course frame significant questions effectively? Do the readings and sequence of assignments evidence a mind alive to the subject, still grappling with significant issues, drawing on the best contemporary and past scholarship and research? Does the course push beyond the comfortable borders of traditional disciplinary study? Does the faculty member think a lot about pedagogy and the defining terms of the subject? If so, writing on teaching issues can as readily be examined for quality of mind and evidences of intellectual growth as can a piece of traditional research. A paper presented at a regional conference, a lecture for an institutional series, software developed for a course—all these can be looked at as evidence of the faculty member's quality of mind, though none of them might be considered as evidence of productivity. But intellectual work should not be treated like so many widgets turned out on an assembly line. Supporting scholarship that does not always result in a tangible product, said Eble and McKeachie (1985), "requires some faith in the internal development of the person and more effort to measure actual impact upon teaching. Yet such development may be fully as important as developing scholarly competence leading to published work" (p. 133).

Can assessment of scholarship (as distinguished now from research) actually work? Good assessment begins with asking the right questions, knowing why they are right, and being open to whatever kinds of information will answer those questions. We always find ways to evaluate what is important to us—not with perfect accuracy but with the degree of precision that is appropriate to the subject being studied. Introducing his *Nichomachean Ethics,* Aristotle said that the well-schooled person is "one who searches for that degree of precision in each kind of study which the nature of the subject at hand admits." If we want to know about intellectual process, we should avoid the false precision of counting only a limited number of its products.

Fortunately, we have models that show us how scholarship can be more effectively assessed. In their review of performance appraisal, Blackburn and Pitney (1988) outline the conditions that make for effective appraisal plans, recommend a specific plan, and cite examples of educational institutions successfully using these approaches. They show that to be effective or fair, performance appraisal must be individualized, since there is so little agreement within or across disciplines of what constitutes scholarship or research. The individual must be directly involved in the design and implementation of the appraisal system, and both the place of work and the discipline must be taken into account as affecting the plan. As all students of evaluation agree, multiple sources of information are essential, including self-evaluation, peer evaluation, student evaluation of teaching, and outside evaluators. Evaluations may need to be designed to meet both administrative purposes and the individual's development needs, but those functions may need to be separated for some individuals. One of the key assumptions behind a plan, Blackburn and Pitney argue, must be that what is good for the faculty member's professional goals is also good for the institution. They conclude their study with the recommendation that institutions wishing to develop effective appraisal systems for faculty performance in teaching, scholarship, and service develop a "portfolio approach."

The Blackburn and Pitney study gives particular attention to the example of Gordon College, which since 1976 has had a voluntary program of growth contracts for its faculty. Each faculty member who elects to enter the plan begins by writing a profile that contains an assessment of strengths and weaknesses, an outline of present roles and an assessment of effectiveness in fulfilling them, and a statement of personal and professional goals for a three- to five-year period. This profile forms the basis for yearly development plans to fulfill the long-range plan. Each yearly plan sets specific goals and the intended means to accomplish and assess each goal. The participant chooses an advisory committee of faculty colleagues, whose purpose is to help the participant refine the growth plan, to give advice during the year, and then to write an assessment of the achievement of goals to accompany the participant's self-evaluation at the end of the year (Carlberg, 1988a, 1988b). Since its inception, 75 percent of the Gordon College faculty have regularly elected to participate in the plan. Among the factors the college identifies as possibly contributing to the positive results of the growth plan are that the program is "faculty owned," that individual faculty "control the direction and thrust of their development," and that the approach is "supportive, not critical." "An individual development plan provides a structure which generates concrete evidence that a productive professional life exists. Fuzz is blowing away; the picture becomes focused" (Carlberg, 1988b, p. 17).

The summary report (Carlberg, 1988a) of the Gordon College plan briefly digests a study by a research team from the University of Michigan Center for the Study of Higher Education. Among the findings are that Gordon College faculty are traditional in the ways they conduct their scholarship and are more likely than colleagues at other institutions to write.

The Gordon College program is perhaps the best known in the country and probably the most detailed in its approach. Furman University and Austin College are two other institutions that have instituted their own programs in professional growth planning (Bedsole, 1983). Earlham College does not have a growth contract plan, but among its supports for professional development are a rotating position for a faculty consultant on teaching and learning and five-year posttenure evaluations for all faculty. Both these programs have been in place since 1975. The faculty consultant can and often does work with faculty to identify scholarly activities to enhance their professional lives and teaching effectiveness. The five-year reviews, which are shaped according to the individual faculty member's agenda for review of professional accomplishments and goal setting for the next five years, involve self-evaluation, peer evaluation, and student evaluation of teaching (Bakker and Lacey, 1980).

These programs are costly to do well. Collegiality is costly; apart from everything else, to institute these programs, a lot of people would have to read each other's writing. There appears to be ample evidence, however, that the benefits accruing to individual faculty members and their institutions from these programs will outweigh the costs.

Conclusion

For most teachers in higher education in this country, scholarly work, rather than traditional disciplinary research leading to publication, is the appropriate means to remain vitalized as teachers and practitioners in their fields. Moreover, such work can be and is being effectively assessed for both personal development purposes and for administrative purposes in granting tenure and making promotion and salary determinations. If those who insist that research leading to publication is essential for every teacher do so because they believe it alone can be effectively and fairly assessed, the evidence should both disturb them, as it reveals the shortcomings in present assessment of research productivity, and set their minds at rest, as it shows how both scholarly and research activities can be evaluated.

References

Bakker, G., and Lacey, P. A. "Faculty Consultants at Earlham." In W. C. Nelsen and M. Siegel, eds., *Effective Approaches to Faculty Development*. Washington, D.C.: Association of American Colleges, 1980.

Bedsole, D. T. (ed.). *Critical Aspects of Faculty Development Programs*. Sherman, Tex.: Center for Program and Institutional Renewal, 1983.

Blackburn, R. T., and Pitney, J. A. *Performance Appraisal for Faculty: Implications for Higher Education*. Ann Arbor, Mich.: National Center for Research to Improve Postsecondary Teaching and Learning, 1988.

Boyer, E. L. *College: The Undergraduate Experience in America*. New York: Harper & Row, 1988.

Carlberg, R. J. (ed.). "Professional Development Through Growth Plans: A Summary Report." Wenham, Mass.: Gordon College, 1988a.

Carlberg, R. J. "Professional Development Through Growth Plans: Gordon College Faculty Development Handbook." Wenham, Mass.: Gordon College, 1988b.

Carnegie Foundation for the Advancement of Teaching. *The Condition of the Profes-*

soriate: Attitudes and Trends—A Technical Report. Princeton, N.J.: Carnegie Foundation for the Advancement of Teaching, 1989.

Ceci, S. J., and Young, R. "Peer Review: A Study of Reliability." *Change,* 1982, *14* (6), 44-48.

Centra, J. A. *Determining Faculty Effectiveness: Assessing Teaching, Research, and Service for Personnel Decisions and Improvement.* San Francisco: Jossey-Bass, 1979.

Clark, B. R. *The Academic Life: Small Worlds, Different Worlds.* Princeton, N.J.: Carnegie Foundation for the Advancement of Teaching, 1987.

Eble, K. E. *Professors as Teachers.* San Francisco: Jossey-Bass, 1972.

Eble, K. E. *The Aims of College Teaching.* San Francisco: Jossey-Bass, 1983.

Eble, K. E. *The Craft of Teaching: A Guide to Mastering the Professor's Art.* (2nd ed.) San Francisco: Jossey-Bass, 1988.

Eble, K. E., and McKeachie, W. J. *Improving Undergraduate Education Through Faculty Development: An Analysis of Effective Programs and Practices.* San Francisco: Jossey-Bass, 1985.

Feldman, K. A. "Research Productivity and Scholarly Accomplishment of College Teachers as Related to Their Instructional Effectiveness: A Review and Exploration." *Research in Higher Education,* 1987, pp. 227-298.

Gastron, J., Lantz, H., and Snyder, C. "Publication Criterion for Promotion in Ph.D. Graduate Departments." *American Sociologist,* 1975, *10,* 239-242.

Lacey, P. A. "Faculty Development and the Future of College Teaching." In R. E. Young and K. E. Eble (eds.), *College Teaching and Learning: Preparing for New Commitments.* New Directions for Teaching and Learning, no. 33. San Francisco: Jossey-Bass, 1988.

Lacey, P. A. "Let's Not Perpetuate Our Mistakes of the Past as We Prepare a New Professorial Generation." *Chronicle of Higher Education,* April 18, 1990, pp. B1, B3.

"Research Focus: Teaching vs. Research—Nature of the Relationship." *The Teaching Professor,* 1989, *3* (1), 7-8.

Soderberg, L. O. "Dominance of Research and Publication: An Unrelenting Tyranny." *College Teaching,* 1985, *33* (4), 168-172.

Weaver, F. S. "Scholarship for the Teaching Faculty." *College Teaching,* 1986, *34* (2), 51-58.

Paul A. Lacey is professor of English of Earlham College, Richmond, Indiana.

Writing assignments for students must seem relevant to their work in college as well as to the outside world.

Kenneth Eble on Writing in College: Ahead of His Time

William J. McCleary

> Making assignments is among the most difficult of a teacher's routine duties. We know the worth of what we ask the students to do, but for students, almost any assignment may seem to be busywork if they don't see what purpose it serves.
> —Eble, 1988b.

"In general, the term paper is a bad assignment," wrote Kenneth Eble in the first edition of *The Craft of Teaching,* published in 1977. And he hadn't changed his mind for the second edition, published in 1988. Of course, the advice was no longer heretical in 1988 because so many advocates of writing across the curriculum (WAC) were saying the same thing. But Eble's saying it in the seventies, before the current revival of WAC began, shows how his views on the important subject of writing in college were just as sane and forward-looking as his other views on college teaching.

Although Eble discussed writing in other articles and books, a chapter of *The Craft of Teaching* entitled "Assignments" summarizes his views on writing and is virtually the same in the two editions; it is the main source for this chapter. Citations here are all from the second edition.

Since Eble died shortly before the second edition of *The Craft of Teaching* was published, the book will remain the final word on the subject of writing in college by an English professor who carved out a "second spe-

---

A shorter version of this chapter appeared in the *Composition Chronicle: Newsletter for Writing Teachers,* December 1988.

cialty" by writing about higher education. As an English professor at the University of Utah, he not only specialized in William Dean Howells and F. Scott Fitzgerald but also taught composition and drew several of his favorite anecdotes from his composition classes. And as a University Professor he wrote extensively on teaching, administration, and faculty development. Along with Wilbert McKeachie of the University of Michigan, he was among the few experienced professors to offer advice on teaching to other professors—a group of people who usually act as if they don't need advice on how to teach. (It is one of the ironies of American education that elementary and secondary teachers are required to learn how to teach but those who teach them are not.)

Why Term Papers Are Not Useful

By opposing term papers, Eble agreed with what the WAC movement would later say about there being better ways of accomplishing the same purposes. He agreed with the aims of the term paper but registered five complaints against it as it is actually used by teachers (Eble, 1988b, p. 133):

- Teachers rarely think through their reasons for assigning papers.
- Too much weight in the course is given to the term paper.
- It is too easy for students to get term papers done for them by someone else.
- Students often face too many papers within a brief term to do any of them justice.
- Faculty members don't provide the feedback that serious written work deserves.

While Eble acknowledged that some of these problems could be partially overcome if faculty members were simply willing to work harder (for example, by supervising the writing of the papers), he preferred using other types of assignments.

The main alternative he suggested is for the teacher to pose specific questions, "indicate where answers might be found, and move students to the legwork that accompanies real investigation. As a practical matter, shorter, focused assignments in which the teacher's expertise plays a significant part offer more chances for learning than term papers do" (1988b, p. 135).

Relevance of Writing and Teaching

With this type of assignment, Eble (1983) was connecting writing to what he had to say about teaching in general in *The Aims of College Teaching*. In that book he questioned the value of simply *having* knowledge, and he attacked the notion that the professor's job is to hand out "packages of knowledge" with no regard to the *use* of knowledge. As he put it, "we live our lives within some crucial and common frameworks—earning a living, establishing a community, maintaining our health, preserving our lives, arriving at a satisfying self-identity; all of what we know or wish to know relates crucially to these" (p. 99). And if education does not relate to these, he said, it's not worth much. Therefore, he concluded, professors must reduce the number of packages of knowledge presented in order to include time for letting students use the knowledge.

This view again fits right into the mold of writing across the curriculum. One strong reason that teachers of all levels resist including writing is that they feel compelled to cover their topic. But knowing is worthless without the use of knowledge, Eble said, and writing is one of the primary ways that knowledge can be put to use in the classroom. Students can be given real or hypothetical problems to solve and can not only explain their solutions in writing but can also argue for these solutions.

Finally, in his essay, "Educating Ritas," Eble (1985) advocated yet another aspect of writing across the curriculum—educating the professors themselves about writing by having them do more writing. He said, "This would enable more teachers to be, in some degree, teachers of writing and to encourage in their students the thinking and feeling that are inseparable aspects of literary expression" (p. 47). He was not speaking of academic writing here but of writing that is "exploratory and engaging, of both the self and the world—writing that searches through the vastness of any human experience and tries hard to find words to express some part of it" (p. 47).

Where did Eble come by this appreciation for writing in all disciplines? Perhaps it came from a study that he and McKeachie (1985) conducted in the early eighties of a faculty development program in the upper Midwest. They discovered that while professors themselves set the highest value on getting out of their institutions to attend conferences or conduct research, supervisors of the faculty development programs at individual institutions said that WAC had the most beneficial impact on undergraduate education. WAC programs, the supervisors told Eble and McKeachie, taught faculty how to increase their efficiency in dealing with student papers, increased faculty competence in both teaching and in their own writing, changed curriculum objectives and instructional methods, and brought about more interdisciplinary activities.

The Advantages of Collaborative Writing

In addition to supporting WAC, Eble was ahead of modern trends in advocating another approach to education and to writing instruction that has become standard among composition teachers—group work. He (1988b) asked, "Why can't a group of students be charged with researching any of the hundreds of problems that professional societies, citizens' groups, public commissions face every day and contributing something to that problem's solution?" (p. 135). He pointed out that many public problems are addressed by groups rather than by individuals. Thus, as he said at another point, Eble was suggesting that teachers "modify the prevailing individualistic competitive model for learning by embracing more cooperation and group effort." In *The Aims of College Teaching* (1983), he described several examples of what could be done:

> A report prepared by a class on actual conditions in a single public school could be as illuminating to a community as the overview gathered together by a national commission. Finding out about the dimensions of child abuse or difficulties faced by the handicapped or the extent of environmental damage of many kinds could be a first step to linking actuality with theory and book learning, again as a means of arriving at a group report that might indeed affect those to whom it was addressed [p. 147].

In English composition courses, this is called collaborative writing, a phrase popularized by collaboration's best-known advocate, Kenneth Bruffee (1973) of Brooklyn College. Eble carried Bruffee's cause one step further by applying its use to writing in other disciplines.

Handwritten Papers

Finally, Eble seems to have anticipated future trends in composition by adopting a third modern belief about the overall gains to be derived from writing. Again, in *The Craft of Teaching* (1988b), he favored handwritten papers, on the grounds that "writing is muscular as well as mental" (p. 138). This view echoes composition teachers who have adopted ideas from cognitive psychology. For example, the authors of one of the most innovative college writing textbooks (Lauer and others, 1981) advised students that writing is so useful because it is "multimodal"—that is, it involves using the muscles (motor concepts), working with visual images (iconic concepts), and working with verbal symbols (semantic concepts). Therefore, Eble (1988b) was not enamored of word processing, "which tends to increase length without necessarily increasing quality" (p. 138). (No, he had not in the first edition anticipated the personal computer; his advice on word processing is the only major revision to the "Assignments" chapter for the second edition.)

Along the same line, Eble also favored having teachers help students see long papers in terms of manageable "blocks of material" in order to simplify the writing task. Word processing is not bad for moving blocks of material around, he acknowledged.

Other Views

Eble had much more than this to say about writing, of course. For example, he suggested that the traditional essay—seldom used outside of composition class—is a worthwhile assignment for other classes. And perhaps most important, he (1988b) demanded that college teachers treat student writing with respect, saying, "Teachers who expect good written work are obligated to read it promptly and well." He accepted no excuses for doing otherwise: "There is no way to require assignments without committing oneself to responding to them" (p. 139).

However, there is no need to repeat here a chapter that should be required reading for every teacher. Nor do we have space to go into other positions that Eble took that relate to teaching composition, such as his attack on the imbalance between teaching and research at research institutions and the pernicious effect this imbalance has on faculty hired only to teach—a group that includes composition teachers above all. Eble (1988a) elaborates on these ideas in "The Contexts of College Teaching." Suffice it to say that Kenneth Eble made contributions to the teaching and use of writing in college that mirror his sensible attitudes toward college teaching in general. The teaching profession will miss him.

References

Bruffee, K. "Collaborative Learning: Some Practical Models." *College English*, 1973, 34 (6), 634-643.

Eble, K. E. *The Aims of College Teaching*. San Francisco: Jossey-Bass, 1983.

Eble, K. E. "Educating Ritas: A Different Kind of Competence." *Educational Horizons*, 1985, 63, 45-48.

Eble, K. E. "The Contexts of College Teaching—Past and Future." In R. E. Young and K. E. Eble (eds.), *College Teaching and Learning: Preparing for New Commitments*. New Directions for Teaching and Learning, no. 33. San Francisco: Jossey-Bass, 1988a.

Eble, K. E. *The Craft of Teaching: A Guide to Mastering the Professor's Art.* (2nd ed.) San Francisco: Jossey-Bass, 1988b.

Eble, K. E., and McKeachie, W. J. *Improving Undergraduate Education Through Faculty Development: An Analysis of Effective Programs and Practices*. San Francisco: Jossey-Bass, 1985.

Lauer, J., and others. *Four Worlds of Writing*. New York: Harper & Row, 1981.

William J. McCleary is editor of Composition Chronicle: Newsletter for Writing Teachers *and teaches English at the State University of New York College, Geneseo.*

Guidelines for creating faculty development programs need to be devised in order to encourage teamwork in curricular design, to assist in faculty evaluations, and to prepare faculty for changing demographic patterns.

The Bush Foundation's Faculty Development Projects

Humphrey Doermann

> There have been few research attempts to conceptualize faculty development. This lack may help explain the absence of comprehensive faculty development plans. With no clear conception of how a faculty develops, an institution may continue to do only elementary things basic to the operation of the institution. But conceptualizing faculty development is not an impossible task. Practical inquiries can be made as to the characteristics of a specific college faculty and as to the continuing research which might provide a sounder basis for action by all institutions.
> —Eble, 1972.

Between 1980 and 1988, Kenneth Eble was one of the principal architects of the Bush Foundation's regional programs in faculty development. The Bush Foundation is predominantly a regional grant-making foundation, which spends about $15 million annually in education, the arts, health, human services, and in several midcareer individual fellowship programs. Most of the money is spent in Minnesota, North Dakota, and South Dakota. The largest single cluster of grants is in higher education.

By the year 2000, these programs will spend in total approximately $27 million in sixty two-year and four-year public and private undergraduate colleges in Minnesota and the Dakotas, and during a ten-year period will spend an additional $8 million of Bush Foundation and Hewlett Foundation money at twenty-five historically black private colleges in the Southeast.

Neither Eble nor the people at the Bush Foundation guessed in 1980 how large and durable these programs would be or how varied and important would be Eble's own contribution toward these results.

The Bush staff in 1979 was inexperienced in faculty development. Knowledgeable advisers had identified faculty development as an area in which the foundation could make an important regional contribution and had helped the staff write initial program guidelines. The foundation's board of directors approved the guidelines in April 1979, and they were then mailed to the eligible four-year colleges in Minnesota, North Dakota, and South Dakota. Proposals flowed in after about six months. The foundation people were willing to get to work but not exactly sure how.

Eble was the first among several consultants asked by Bush staff members to accompany them on visits to applicant colleges and to review individual grant applications. Eble's other tasks, never formally stated, were to help the staff define what its rather general guidelines should mean in a wide variety of individual circumstances and, more generally, to help the staff learn how to exercise common sense in faculty development.

Faculty Development: A Definition

The definition of faculty development that Eble encountered in the foundation's guidelines was and still is quite broad in order to provide freedom for the local design of specific grant projects. The guidelines included in their definition individual professional development, instructional development, curriculum development, and organizational development. Individual professional development activity could include sabbatical supplements or minigrant programs that permit individual faculty members to begin or pursue small-scale research projects. Examples of instructional development activity include programs of workshops directed at improving teaching or the establishment of campus teaching and learning centers. Curriculum development could involve general faculty examination of major academic sectors, such as general education, or installation of such programs as writing across the curriculum. Organizational development might deal with such questions as improving student evaluation of courses or experimenting with external peer review of departmental offerings—usually in conjunction with already mandated internal self-studies.

While the Bush program spent money for faculty activity, the central long-run purpose was improvement of student learning. The Bush program guidelines asked each applicant college to say what student learning problems or opportunities it chose to work on and why, how this in turn led to the selected faculty development strategy in the Bush grant proposal, and how the college might know later what happened as a result and whether it was worthwhile. Some colleges chose to spend money on a single project or plan, while others designed cafeteria-style programs with a variety of optional components.

Individual colleges could apply for an initial planning grant of up to $10,000, followed by up to two three-year program grants whose maximum annual payments varied from $25,000 a year to $300,000 a year depending on the size of undergraduate enrollment.

The Grant-Making Process and Its Evaluation

During the early pregrant site visits, Eble's approach to gathering information and reaching judgments soon began to influence how the foundation staff approached the work. In the beginning, the staff was inclined to ask what faculty development strategies work best and which ones work badly, and then to try to apply those norms in judging whether a particular application made sense. Eble postponed such judgments, insisting first that the reviewers understand each particular situation—how each proposal was generated, in response to which locally identified needs, with whose initiative and whose subsequent involvement.

On Bush Foundation site visits, without insulting administrators, Eble made clear his primary respect for faculty initiative and faculty leadership in planning faculty development activities. While showing no disrespect to the pursuit of original scholarship, he made clear in many ways his determination that enthusiastic teaching should not have lesser status. He was skeptical of quick-fix plans and of occasional suggestions that appeared to arise from individual self-interest rather than objective analysis. For the faculty planning groups in the colleges involved, Eble's Bush Foundation site visits usually brought welcome affirmation and only occasionally mild unease.

In 1983 and 1984, Eble and Wilbert J. McKeachie (1985) conducted a major evaluation of the initial Bush program of faculty development grants in Minnesota and the Dakotas. The study described the various locally developed faculty development strategies being pursued by participating colleges in these states. It assessed the strengths and weaknesses of these strategies and made significant recommendations for the scope and future direction of the foundation's faculty development work.

Before writing the evaluation, Eble and McKeachie examined many kinds of information about the forty-one colleges that were actively participating in 1983 and 1984. Most of those colleges had operated for two or three years under an initial Bush faculty development program grant. The Bush Foundation files contained proposals for each participating college along with annual progress and expenditure reports. Eble and McKeachie arranged to visit the colleges, going together as a team in about a third of the cases and alone otherwise. They spoke with the faculty planning groups most closely involved in supervising the Bush-supported activities and with other faculty who might or might not have participated in those activities. They talked with administrators and with students and visited classes. McKeachie conducted a 12 percent random sample questionnaire survey among faculty at the participating colleges, seeking views about the satisfactions and drawbacks of their current teaching situation as well as data and attitudes about faculty development activity. Ninety percent of the faculty in the survey responded (excluding those on leave or otherwise away from campus).

From these sources of information, Eble and McKeachie determined that a majority of faculty in the surveyed colleges participated in the Bush-supported faculty development activities. Partly as a result of this participation, the faculty norms were changing as to what was perceived as good teaching. The most noticeable change of this kind was the increased attention given by faculty in many colleges to improvement of student writing throughout the curriculum. Since much of the planning for this activity was faculty-based in the first instance, the Bush program probably accelerated these developments but had not initiated them. Conversations with administrators and faculty confirmed that the Bush projects frequently stimulated greater long-run budgetary commitment to faculty development programs than had existed previously. The McKeachie questionnaire survey found relatively high faculty morale and job satisfaction within the colleges sampled, significantly higher than those reported from recent prior national surveys. This finding seemed important in understanding the context of their joint review, even though no cause-and-effect relationship was established between high morale and the relatively large amount of faculty development work taking place.

Characteristics of Successful Faculty Development Activities

One part of Eble and McKeachie's (1985) conclusions differentiated the effectiveness of the Bush program among types of faculty development activity and among groups of participating colleges and universities:

> Our analysis suggests that even though grants for individual scholarly activities are valued, curricular change, workshops, and other programs involving faculty members working together to achieve common objectives may be more cost effective for the institution in terms of their impact on student learning. . . . Curriculum change and instructional development [activities] emerged as more successful than we expected, and faculty grants, while useful, seemed to be less cost effective in their impact upon education. . . .
>
> Overall, our results support the conclusion that the Bush grants had the greatest impact on the smaller, less prestigious, less affluent institutions [p. 205].

The authors also identified general characteristics of the most successful Bush-supported faculty development programs at individual colleges:

- They were careful and complete in their planning.
- They offered neither too extensive a cafeteria nor were too focused on limited objectives. The diversity of opportunities recognized a diversity of faculty needs and interests but still maintained a program identity.
- They had effective leadership from both faculty and administrators without diminishing the feeling of faculty ownership of the program.
- They enlisted substantial numbers of faculty in planning and administering the program; the institution and the program were well suited to one another.
- They were not initiated in ways that threatened the faculty or increased insecurity.
- They did not aim at "deadwood" or "developing" those who had been ineffective but rather offered opportunities for the solid, substantial contributors as well as the "stars" or the alienated; they gave the faculty a sense that they were valued.
- They stimulated faculty enthusiasm and a high rate of participation of the faculty in various aspects of the program.
- They created situations in which faculty members felt increased colleague support for investments in teaching and a greater sense that administrators valued teaching.
- They had a visibility on campus among faculty and, to some degree, among students, beyond being known to those who directly benefited from the program.
- They took account of time pressure, inviting greater investment but not demanding permanent additions to the faculty work load.
- The activities of the program resulted in tangible changes in courses, teaching strategies, subject matter competence, curricula, and the like from which reasonable inferences could be made as to improving student learning.
- They provided training to develop new skills, not just exhortation.
- The activities increased interaction and communication among faculty and students in working toward common goals. At the highest degree of success, the program created a better climate for teaching and learning; commitment to teaching and communicating about teaching became normative.
- The program took risks; it challenged the faculty to stretch individual efforts and to see beyond their own professional growth toward its impact on both students and the institution [pp. 216-217].

Expansion of the Program

In their advice to the Bush Foundation board of directors, Eble and McKeachie advocated continuing the Bush program within its three-state geographic region and suggested that the foundation program guidelines emphasize those aspects that earlier had proved to be most successful. The authors favored extending Bush program eligibility to community colleges, two-year tribally controlled American Indian colleges, and into other regions or collegiate sectors as well. They noted that a major new generation of college faculty would be hired during the 1990s and believed that specific program attention should be devoted to giving these teachers a successful start in their work. Finally, Eble and McKeachie observed that the college students of the future will be more diverse as to age and background than in the past. Colleges today, they said, should try to understand better this new population and what its diversity may imply in the future for effective teaching and learning.

Members of the foundation program staff agreed with Eble's judgment that many of the faculty development activities being carried out in four-year colleges in Minnesota and the Dakotas might also be important in two-year colleges, in the American Indian two-year tribally controlled colleges on reservations, and in historically black private colleges where the foundation already operated other programs. The board of directors encouraged exploration of these possibilities by foundation staff members at the same time Eble and McKeachie were forming their final recommendations and publishing them. By 1986 the foundation board had approved extension of its faculty development programs into all of these areas and had begun to approve program grants.

During the last three years of his life, Eble successfully recommended approval of faculty development grants at these American Indian colleges: Sinte Gleska College Center, Rosebud, South Dakota; Standing Rock Community College, Fort Yates, North Dakota; Turtle Mountain Community College, Belcourt, North Dakota; Blackfeet Community College, Browning, Montana; Oglala Lakota College, Kyle, South Dakota; and Navajo Community College, Tsaile, Arizona. Similarly, he participated in grants to these historically black private four-year colleges: Benedict College, Columbia, South Carolina; Claflin College, Orangeburg, South Carolina; Morehouse College, Atlanta, Georgia; Talladega College, Talladega, Alabama; and Voorhees College, Denmark, South Carolina.

By October 1988, Eble had participated in forty-five site visits to review individual pregrant proposals and in five consultant conferences to review general progress in the Bush program and to suggest changes in its design. He had become a significant program adviser for the whole Bush staff and board of directors.

The Bush Foundation faculty development program that Eble encountered in 1980 was projected to cost about $11 million over eight years among four-year colleges in a three-state region. With his guidance and encouragement, the program expanded greatly in scope and length and will receive at least $35 million over an eighteen-year span. During the past ten years, this program represented the largest single area of Bush Foundation emphasis, occupying approximately 11 percent of the foundation's total grant spending.

References

Eble, K. E. *Professors as Teachers.* San Francisco: Jossey-Bass, 1972.

Eble, K. E., and McKeachie, W. J. *Improving Undergraduate Education Through Faculty Development: An Analysis of Effective Programs and Practices.* San Francisco: Jossey-Bass, 1985.

Humphrey Doermann is president of the Bush Foundation, Saint Paul, Minnesota.

INDEX

Academe, 13-14
"Academic Dogma", 41
Achebe, C., 47, 50, 52
Adams, H., 12, 13, 19
Affirmative action, for recruiting faculty, 41
African history, 39-40
Althusser, L., 62, 71
American Association for the Advancement of Science, 15
American Association of University Professors (AAUP), 3
American Indian colleges, grants for, 112
Appiah, K., 39-40
Aristotle, 97
Association of American Colleges, 3
Athletics, role of, 17-18
Attrition rates, of blacks, 34
Austin College, 98
Authoritarianism, in the classroom, 69

Bacon, F., 35
Baily, M. N., 83, 88
Bakker, G., 99
Baldwin, J., 36-37, 43
Barbour, D. H., 83, 88
Barzun, J., 15
Beck, C. E., 87, 88
Bedsole, D. T., 98, 99
Belcher, G., 52
Bennet, W. J., 7, 9, 61
Bernhardt, 85, 86, 87-88
Black America, history of, 39
Black private colleges, grants for, 112
Blackburn, R. T., 94-95, 96, 97-98, 99
"Blacks and Whites on the Campuses . . .", 34, 43
Bloom, A., 7, 9, 11-12, 15, 18-19, 35, 41-42, 43, 50, 52, 61, 73-76, 79, 80
Booth, W., 7, 8, 21-31
Bork, R., 11
Bowen, W., 88
Boyer, E. L., 1, 2, 38, 92, 94, 99
Bridges, C. W., 47, 52
Bruffee, K., 104, 105
Buckley, W., 11
Bush era, 73, 74

Bush Foundation, faculty development projects of, 107-113
Bywater, T. R., 8, 73-81

Capitalism, and education, 62-64
Carlberg, R. J., 98, 99
Carnegie Corporation, 3
Carnegie Foundation for the Advancement of Teaching, 12, 13, 38, 92, 99-100
Carter era, 74
Ceci, S. J., 95, 100
Centra, J. A., 95, 100
Cheney, L. V., 6-7, 9
Chronicle of Higher Education, 5, 15, 33, 43
Civil rights, attacks on, 61-62
Clark, B. R., 92, 93-94, 100
Collaborative learning, 53-59
Collaborative writing, 103-104
Community colleges, grants for, 111; and humanities education, 73-81; pitfalls of, 79-80; strengths of, 76-79
Comparative literature, widening of, 40
Competition, among institutions, 5
Composition, teaching of, 45-52. *See also* Writing
Computers, and teaching writing, 83-89, 104
Congressional Research Service, 34
Conservatism, effects of, 7, 34, 61-62, 74-75. *See also* Bush era, Reagan era
Core curricula, and teaching cultural diversity, 38, 45-52
Corporate interests, effects of, 62-64, 79
Cultural diversity, in educational institutions, 5, 7, 45-52. *See also* Cultural geneticism, Cultural literacy, Multiculturalism
Cultural geneticism, 35-37. *See also* Cultural diversity, Multiculturalism
Cultural literacy, 37-38, 46, 49-50, 61-71
Cultural nationalism, 37
Curriculum development, 108

Dalton, D. W., 87, 88
Deliberalization, of education, 21-31

115

Denham, R., 14, 19
Department of Defense, research of, 12
Development program, in community college, 78
Dewey, J., 42–43
Diedrich scale, and evaluating writing, 85
Dobberstein, M., 8, 83–87
Doermann, H., 8, 107–113
Du Bois, W.E.B., 37, 43
Duling, R. A., 85, 88

Earlham College, 98–99
Eble, K. E., 1–9, 11–19, 21, 31, 33, 43, 45, 52, 53, 59, 61, 71, 73–76, 79, 80, 81, 83, 89, 91, 93, 97, 100, 101–105, 107–113
Edison, T., 18
Edwards, P., 85, 86, 87–88
Elitism, in institutions, 5, 6, 21–31
English, varieties of, 46–49
Enrollment rates, of blacks, 34
Essays, traditional, 105
Etchison, C., 85, 86, 89
Ethnic studies departments, 41
Evaluation, of scholarship, 96–99
Experimental design, in evaluating computers and writing, 84–87
Experts: and faculty evaluation; and liberal education, 63

Faculty consultants, 99
Faculty development, 91–100, 107–113; in community colleges, 78
Faculty: black, 34–35; and collegiality, 76–77; and scholarship, 91–100; superstar, 14
Federal aid, decline in, 34
Feldman, K. A., 92–93, 100
Fiction, and cultural literacy, 47–49
Fitzgerald, F. S., 7, 102
Foucault, M., 36, 43
Franklin, P., 14, 19
Freedman, D., 86, 89
Freedom, in the classroom, 66–70
Freire, P., 68, 71
Furman University, 98

Gallop poll, on geography, 38
Gandhi, M., 33
Gardner, D. P., 1–2
Gastron, J., 95, 100
Gates, H. L., Jr., 7, 8, 33–44

Geertz, C., 40, 43
German university, 12
Giamatti, A. B., 17
Glazer, N. Y., 68, 71
Goody, J., 39
Gordon College, 98
Graff, G., 42, 43
Gramsci, A., 36, 43
Grant writing, of faculty, 78
Grants, 16–17, 107–113
Grogg, P. M., 85, 87, 89
Growth contracts, for faculty, 98
Guttmann, A., 42, 43

Hancock, L., 64, 71
Handwritten papers, value of, 104. *See also* Computers
Hannafin, M. J., 87, 88
Hawisher, G. E., 84, 85, 86, 87, 89
Hearn, G., 52
Hegemonic pedagogy, and neutrality, 64
Heidegger, M., 36, 43
Helms, J., 61–62
Hewlett Foundation, 107
Hirsch, E. D., Jr., 7, 9, 46, 52, 61
Holistic evaluation, of writing, 85, 86
Homeless, increase of, 74
Honors program, in community college, 78
Howells, W. D., 102
Humanities, decentering of, 38–40, 66–70
Hutchins, R. M., 42, 43

Instructional development, 108
Interdisciplinary courses, 77, 78. *See also* Writing across the curriculum movement
International knowledge, prevalence of, 37–38

Jaeger, R. M., 85, 89
James, W., 13, 14
Jobs, S., 87
John M. Olin Center for Inquiry into the Theory and Practice of Democracy, 73
Johnson, S., 91
Jowett, 35–36
Joyce, J., 50–51
Jussawalla, F., 5–9, 45–52

Kaplan, H., 85, 89
Katz, A., 69, 71
Kimball, R., 61, 71

Lacey, P. A., 8, 91-100
Lantz, H., 95, 100
Lauer, J., 104, 105
Laurence, D., 14, 19
Lessing, D., 95
Literacy, lack of, 74-75
Literary theory, 40
Lunsford, R., 47, 52
Lutz, J. A., 84, 89

Macaulay, 46
McCarthy era, 42
McCleary, W. J., 8, 101-105
McFarland, T., 35-36, 43
McFarlane, 50
McKeatchie, 93, 97, 102, 103, 105, 109-113
Maimon, E., 47, 52
Mandel, E., 63, 71
Mapplethorpe, R., 61
Marcroft, M., 8, 61-71
Marquand, R., 34, 43
Marx, K., 71
Mathesis universalis. See Universal knowledge
Melville, H., 41, 43
Minorities, and education, 33-44
Modern Language Association, 14
Moramarco, F., 7, 9
Multiculturalism, in education, 36-43, 61-71. See also Cultural diversity; Cultural geneticism
Munter, M., 83, 89

Naipaul, V. S., 45, 51, 52
Narayan, R. K., 47-49, 51, 52
National Center of Education Statistics, 34
National Commission on Excellence in Education, 1, 2, 46
National Endowment for the Humanities, 77
National Governors Association, 37-38
Neutrality, ethics of, 64, 68
New York Times, 38, 61
Nisbet, R., 41, 43
Nobine, B., 52

O'Connor, F. W., 52
Oral history, 39
Organizational development, 108

p'Bitek, O., 50, 52
Parameswaran, U., 46, 52

Parry, M., 39, 43
Pearson, P., 83, 89
Pedagogy: oppositional, 61-71; traditional, 64-66
Peer reviews, of faculty, 96
Performance appraisal, of faculty, 97-98
Personal voice, versus transactional voice, 49
Ph.D.s, of blacks, 35
Pisani, R., 86, 89
Pitney, 94-95, 96, 97-98
Pivarnik, B. A., 85, 89
Pluralism, importance of, 42-43
Politics: in the classroom, 64-70; and cultural literacy, 50, 61-71
Poris, M., 85, 86, 89
Poststructuralist pedagogy, 66-68
Presidents, of community colleges, 80
Press, R. M., 34, 44
Publishing, by faculty, 6, 78, 92, 95-96. See also Research, Scholarship
Purves, R., 86, 89

Quality of mind, of faculty, 96-97

Racism, on campus, 33-34, 41, 62
Rao, R., 47, 52
Reagan era, effects of, 34, 73, 74, 79
Reed, I., 40-41, 44
Regression, in experimental research, 86
Research papers, writing of, 57-59
Research parks, 15-16, 18
Research universities, 75-76, 79, 80
Research: funding of, 12; and productivity, 96; and scholarship, 91-100; versus teaching, 15-16.
Resources, use of for writing, 57-58
Rosenblatt, R., 61, 71
Rushdie, S., 50-51

Salovey, P., 30
Schneider, C., 21-22
Scholarship, of college teachers, 91-92, 100; defining of, 94-96; evaluation of, 96-100; and teaching, 92-94; 100
Schwartz, E., 85, 86-87, 89
Scott, D., 62
Seeley, J., 19
Semiotic Society of America, 15
Serrano, A., 61-62
Site visits, for grants, 109
Sixties radicalism, 61, 75, 76

Smallen, D. L., 83, 89
Smith, P., 15, 19
Snow, C. P., 38
Snyder, C., 95, 100
Soderberg, L. O., 95, 100
Sommers, E., 85, 86-87, 89
State legislatures, and community colleges, 79
Stibravy, J. A., 87, 88
Student questionnaires, computerized, 5
Study Group on the Condition of Excellence in Higher Education, 1, 2

Tagore, 51
Teaching: flight from, 12-15; and scholarship, 92-94; women versus men in, 13
Technologism, 63
Teichman, M., 85, 86, 89
Tenure, granting of, 5-6, 92, 95, 99
Term papers, limitations of, 102
Third world literature, 5; in composition classrooms, 7-8, 46-52
Thoreau, H. D., 2
Trickle-down theory, 74, 75
Turner, V., 40
Tutuola, A., 49, 52

Ulmer, G. L., 66, 71
Undergraduate education, quality of, 1, 11-19, 21-31, 73-81
Universal knowledge, concept of, 35-36, 38
University of California, Berkeley, 34

University of California, and loyalty oaths, 42
University of Chicago, 11
University of Texas at El Paso (UTEP), 7, 49
University of Utah, 1, 3
University of Virginia, 5

Varner, I. I., 85, 87, 89
Vocational training, in community colleges, 79
Vockell, E. L., 85, 86-87, 89

Walkerdine, V., 65, 71
Walsh, A., 8, 53-59
Weaver, F. S., 94, 95, 100
Weir, A. L., 48, 52
Weiss, T., 85, 86-87, 89
Wojahn, P., 85, 86, 87-88
Wojnarowicz, D., 62
Woolley, W. C., 85, 89
Word processors. *See* Computers
Wright, R., 37, 43
Writers, bilingual, 46-52
Writing across the curriculum movement (WAC), 47, 49, 101-103, 108, 110
Writing, teaching of, 53-59, 83-89, 101-105. *See also* Composition, Writing across the curriculum movement

Young, R., 95, 100

Zavarzadeh, M., 64, 71

Ordering Information

NEW DIRECTIONS FOR TEACHING AND LEARNING is a series of paperback books that presents ideas and techniques for improving college teaching, based both on the practical expertise of seasoned instructors and on the latest research findings of educational and psychological researchers. Books in the series are published quarterly in Fall, Winter, Spring, and Summer and are available for purchase by subscription as well as by single copy.

SUBSCRIPTIONS for 1990 cost $39.00 for individuals (a savings of 20 percent over single-copy prices) and $52.00 for institutions, agencies, and libraries. Please do not send institutional checks for personal subscriptions. Standing orders are accepted.

SINGLE COPIES cost $13.95 when payment accompanies order. (California, New Jersey, New York, and Washington, D.C., residents please include appropriate sales tax.) Billed orders will be charged postage and handling.

DISCOUNTS FOR QUANTITY ORDERS are available. Please write to the address below for information.

ALL ORDERS must include either the name of an individual or an official purchase order number. Please submit your order as follows:
 Subscriptions: specify series and year subscription is to begin
 Single copies: include individual title code (such as TL1)

MAIL ALL ORDERS TO:
 Jossey-Bass Inc., Publishers
 350 Sansome Street
 San Francisco, California 94104

FOR SALES OUTSIDE OF THE UNITED STATES CONTACT:
 Maxwell Macmillan International Publishing Group
 866 Third Avenue
 New York, New York 10022

OTHER TITLES AVAILABLE IN THE
NEW DIRECTIONS FOR TEACHING AND LEARNING SERIES
Robert E. Young, Editor-in-Chief

TL43 Student Ratings of Instruction: Issues for Improving Practice, *Michael Theall, Jennifer Franklin*
TL42 The Changing Face of College Teaching, *Marilla D. Svinicki*
TL41 Learning Communities: Creating Connections Among Students, Faculty, and Disciplines, *Faith Gabelnick, Jean MacGregor, Roberta S. Matthews, Barbara Leigh Smith*
TL40 Integrating Liberal Learning and Professional Education, *Robert A. Armour, Barbara S. Fuhrmann*
TL39 Teaching Assistant Training in the 1990s, *Jody D. Nyquist, Robert D. Abbott*
TL38 Promoting Inquiry in Undergraduate Learning, *Frederick Stirton Weaver*
TL37 The Department Chairperson's Role in Enhancing College Teaching, *Ann F. Lucas*
TL36 Strengthening Programs for Writing Across the Curriculum, *Susan H. McLeod*
TL35 Knowing and Doing: Learning Through Experience, *Pat Hutchings, Allen Wutzdorff*
TL34 Assessing Students' Learning, *Robert E. Young, Kenneth E. Eble*
TL33 College Teaching and Learning: Preparing for New Commitments, *Robert E. Young, Kenneth E. Eble*
TL32 Teaching Large Classes Well, *Maryellen Gleason Weimer*
TL31 Techniques for Evaluating and Improving Instruction, *Lawrence M. Aleamoni*
TL30 Developing Critical Thinking and Problem-Solving Abilities, *James E. Stice*
TL29 Coping with Faculty Stress, *Peter Seldin*
TL28 Distinguished Teachers on Effective Teaching, *Peter G. Beidler*
TL27 Improving Teacher Education, *Eva C. Galambos*
TL26 Communicating in College Classrooms, *Jean M. Civikly*
TL25 Fostering Academic Excellence Through Honors Programs, *Paul G. Friedman, Reva Jenkins-Friedman*
TL24 College-School Collaboration: Appraising the Major Approaches, *William T. Daly*
TL23 Using Research to Improve Teaching, *Janet C. Donald, Arthur M. Sullivan*
TL22 Strengthening the Teaching Assistant Faculty, *John D. W. Andrews*
TL21 Teaching as Though Students Mattered, *Joseph Katz*
TL20 Rejuvenating Introductory Courses, *Karen I. Spear*
TL19 Teaching and Aging, *Chandra M. N. Mehrotra*
TL18 Increasing the Teaching Role of Academic Libraries, *Thomas G. Kirk*
TL17 The First Year of College Teaching, *L. Dee Fink*

TL16 Teaching Minority Students, *James H. Cones III, John F. Noonan, Denise Janha*
TL15 Revitalizing Teaching Through Faculty Development, *Paul A. Lacey*
TL14 Learning in Groups, *Clark Bouton, Russell Y. Garth*
TL12 Teaching Writing in All Disciplines, *C. Williams Griffin*
TL11 Practices That Improve Teaching Evaluation, *Grace French-Lazovik*
TL10 Motivating Professors to Teach Effectively, *James L. Bess*
TL9   Expanding Learning Through New Communications Technologies, *Christopher K. Knapper*
TL3   Fostering Critical Thinking, *Robert E. Young*
TL2   Learning, Cognition, and College Teaching, *Wilbert J. McKeachie*
TL1   Improving Teaching Styles, *Kenneth E. Eble*

STATEMENT OF OWNERSHIP, MANAGEMENT AND CIRCULATION
Required by 39 U.S.C. 3685

1A. Title of Publication: New Directions for Teaching and Learning
1B. Publication No.: 001-801
2. Date of Filing: 9/18/90
3. Frequency of Issue: Quarterly
3A. No. of Issues Published Annually: Four (4)
3B. Annual Subscription Price: $45 individual / $60 institutional
4. Complete Mailing Address of Known Office of Publication: 350 Sansome Street, San Francisco, CA 94104-1310
5. Complete Mailing Address of the Headquarters of General Business Offices of the Publisher: (above address)
6. Full Names and Complete Mailing Address of Publisher, Editor, and Managing Editor:

Publisher: Jossey-Bass Inc., Publishers (above address)

Editor: Robert E. Young, Dean, University of Wisconsin Center, Fox Valley, 1478 Midway Road, Menasha, WI 54952

Managing Editor: Steven Piersanti, President, Jossey-Bass Inc., Publishers (above address)

7. Owner:

Full Name	Complete Mailing Address
Maxwell Communications Corp., plc	Headington Hill Hall, Oxford OX30BW, U.K.

8. Known Bondholders, Mortgagees, and Other Security Holders Owning or Holding 1 Percent or More of Total Amount of Bonds, Mortgages or Other Securities:

Full Name	Complete Mailing Address
same as above	same as above

10. Extent and Nature of Circulation:

	Average No. Copies Each Issue During Preceding 12 Months	Actual No. Copies of Single Issue Published Nearest to Filing Date
A. Total No. Copies	1700	1790
B. Paid and/or Requested Circulation		
1. Sales through dealers and carriers, street vendors and counter sales	367	69
2. Mail Subscription	856	759
C. Total Paid and/or Requested Circulation	1223	828
D. Free Distribution by Mail, Carrier or Other Means, Samples, Complimentary, and Other Free Copies	96	65
E. Total Distribution	1319	893
F. Copies Not Distributed		
1. Office use, left over, unaccounted, spoiled after printing	381	897
2. Return from News Agents	0	0
G. TOTAL	1700	1790

11. I certify that the statements made by me above are correct and complete

Larry Ishii, Vice-President